MANUELA WAGNER • FABIA   AM

TEACHING
Intercultural Citizenship
Across the Curriculum:
THE ROLE OF LANGUAGE EDUCATION

ACTFL
1001 N. Fairfax St.
Suite 200
Alexandria, VA 22314
www.actfl.org

Table of Contents

Acknowledgments

This book is the product of the stimulating environments of many collaborative endeavors in which we have had the good fortune to participate. So we would like to acknowledge the contributions of teachers, school administrators, students, and colleagues who worked with us in other projects. We have learned tremendously from them, and our work with them has inspired and encouraged the work we present here.

We would particularly like to thank the administrators, teachers, and students at West Woods Upper Elementary Schools in Farmington, Connecticut, for opening their classroom doors and sharing their curricula and lesson plans with us, so that together we could develop units for Intercultural Citizenship integrating different school subjects. We are especially grateful to Tara Vazquez, director of the Social Studies and Science curriculum, for facilitating school visits, curriculum access, school presentations, and many other opportunities that enabled the flow of innovative ideas in our group, always with the students' needs and motivations in mind. We are deeply thankful to the graduate students who collaborated with us in this project for developing and providing critical feedback on the interdisciplinary units that have been springboards for some of the examples presented in this book.

In connection with Scenarios A and B in Chapter 1, we thank in particular Madelyn Colonnese (Mathematics Education), Nicole Coleman (German), Kyle Evans (Mathematics), Silke Gräfnitz (German), Steven LeMay (Mathematics), Catherine Maloney (Mathematics), Melissa Scarborough (Language Education), Niko Tracksdorf (German), Deanne Wallace (German), and Carsen Witt (German). We would also like to thank Jocelyn Tamborello-Noble, Deanne Wallace, and Andrea Bohling for our earlier work with them which provided the basis for Scenario C. We are indebted to Dr. Petra Rauschert of Ludwig-Maximilians-Universität in Munich, Germany, for letting us showcase in this book a project she had designed with Dr. Claudia Owczarek, also of Ludwig-Maximilians-Universität in Munich, Germany, and which clearly exemplifies the use of our proposed approach at the university level. We appreciate her generous contribution to Scenario D.

We have benefited greatly from the insights and inquiries from a wide variety of teachers at all educational levels who have interacted with us in different ways in school projects, conferences, personal communications, and social media. Our work presented herein has been strengthened by the questions, concerns and challenges they raised about teaching for Intercultural Citizenship across the disciplines. In particular, we are grateful to Beckie Bray Rankin, Dorie Conlon Perugini, Melina Porto, Caroline Jäger, and Jing Mei for sharing with us their thoughtful questions which resonate with those of many other educators and have become the basis for the FAQ section of Chapter 6.

In addition, we are deeply grateful for the support and encouragement we received from many colleagues in writing this book. We would particularly like to thank: Pete Swanson, for believing in this book and consistently supporting it from the beginning; Paul Sandrock and Sarah Lindstrom, for carefully reviewing chapter drafts and for the thoughtful feedback that helped strengthen our work; and Marty Abbott and Aleidine Moeller, for encouraging and inspiring us through their tireless efforts in promoting the bigger picture in world language education. We are also very grateful to Marty Abbott for accepting our invitation to write a foreword.

We would also like to acknowledge the contribution of the University of Connecticut, specifically Teachers for a New Era and directors Dr. Scott Brown and Dr. Marijke Kehrhahn, who had the vision to support interdisciplinary projects through their words and with funds from the beginning, thereby enabling us to engage in this endeavor. We are grateful to the Neag School of Education and the College of Liberal Arts and Sciences for their support. We thank Dr. Michael Lynch, director of the Humanities Institute, for his interest in our project and his financial support of it through the Humility and Conviction in Public Life project, which was essential in allowing us to broaden the horizons of our work. We are especially grateful to colleagues in our immediate departments (Literatures, Cultures, and Languages and Mathematics), as well as throughout the university for their encouragement throughout the project.

Most of all, we wish to thank our families and friends. The demands of producing this book sometimes overtook family time, and our responsibilities to them had to take second place. So our most heartfelt thanks go to them, not only for allowing us to complete this work but also for representing the most enthusiastic supporters and believers in the importance of educating all students for Intercultural Citizenship.

Foreword

The power of this text lies in the authors' ability to move language educators to provide learning experiences that transcend place and time and have a lasting impact on students. As we face a pivotal moment in advocating for the viability of language programs in the United States, it is critical that, almost 25 years after the release of the *World-Readiness Standards for Learning Languages*, educators persist in making the language classroom a place where the 5 C's still take precedence: Using the language as a communication vehicle for cultural exploration that hinges on understanding the perspectives of those who speak the language while connecting the content from other disciplines to the tasks undertaken, resulting in learners' insight into both their own language and their own culture. And all of these efforts are designed to take student learning beyond the classroom.

It is important that what happens in the language classroom is significant and transformative for learners. As Wagner, Cardetti and Byram espouse, we need to create learning experiences that lead students to "go outside" in order to discover "what's inside." That is, going beyond the confines of the classroom to develop insight into their own attitudes and beliefs that can have a lasting impact on their development not only as language learners but as human beings.

Authors Chip and Dan Heath in their book, *The Power of Moments*, discuss the incredible impact that defining moments have on people and how they can actually be created rather than left to chance. They describe a study of college syllabi as professors were asked to identify the elements from their courses that they hoped students would remember 15-20 years after taking the course. Their responses centered around a lifelong love and appreciation for the discipline as well as lifelong learning in the subject area. When the syllabi were examined, none of them reflected these long-term goals in their course descriptions.

This is the same dilemma we face in language programs when a grammar-based syllabus drives the course content and subsequently drives students away from learning the language. The sample scenarios outlined in this book, mapped against Byram's intercultural framework focusing on knowledge, attitudes, and skills, are powerful templates for creating the kind of learning experiences that will have lasting impact on our learners and give language classrooms the centrality in America's school curricula that is key to understanding our rapidly changing world.

Teaching Intercultural Citizenship Across the Curriculum provides a roadmap that can lead our students to this all important self-reflection and self-awareness. While the authors reference "borders" and "citizenship," which in today's environment can be "red flag terms," they seek to define them in a way that requires a new understanding from the outset. Borders between countries do exist and it is precisely the act of "crossing" these borders that is critical to understanding perspectives that may be different from the ones we know. The use of "citizenship" in the term "Intercultural citizenship" is not referring to allegiance to a specific country in terms of "becoming" a citizen or being born into citizenry but actually embarking on that journey toward global competence that allows students to see themselves as people who can make their way through unfamiliar territory as they experience other cultures and ways of thinking and doing—and do it with a growing sense of comfort and curiosity.

As language educators create a learning environment that invites students, not only to become active investigators of content, but also to freely and respectfully express their opinions and ideas, the language program becomes the pivotal and central place in the curriculum where students feel safe doing so. This is in concert with ACTFL's efforts to highlight this aspect of a language learning experience as etched into the organization's strategic plan resulting in publications and a white paper on Diversity and Inclusion, a major undertaking over the next several years. It is certain that this initiative will not be seen as a short-lived effort culminating in a declaration that the goals have been completed, but a movement that will become an integral part of all of ACTFL's efforts in the language field and beyond.

The language classroom has already become a place where cultural explorations and insights allow challenging and uncomfortable topics to be addressed against the tableau of other cultures and the insights they allow us to draw against some of the historical and current U.S. sentiment. The language classroom can and should be a safe haven where students can express themselves freely and openly and find acceptance and valuing of their personal and ethnic backgrounds as well as their linguistic and cultural heritage. Because language educators have already been on the journey toward intercultural competence, they are well-positioned to establish a microcosm of "intellectual humanity" that will serve learners well for the rest of their life. The language classroom becomes the place where learners can practice the often challenging routes to being courageous. As Chip and Dan Heath describe it in their book on defining moments, "it is hard to be courageous but easier if you have practiced a response." As language educators, we can set up the scenarios where students can practice the courageous responses that will set them on a brave pathway in life.

While the idea of interdisciplinarity has been discussed and promoted in the field for several decades, the fear of having to be the "knower of all information" has resulted in many educators steering clear of implementing such an approach. When the *World-Readiness Standards* were initially released, the Connections Goal area was one of the least embraced goal areas with many educators claiming that they already had infused other subject areas into their curriculum. This was true at the time, as art and music were prominent in most language curricula, and even aspects of the social studies discipline. Very few, however, were embracing the STEM fields, a notion that now is keenly a focus in many schools and universities. The challenges remain, but the need to synthesize the learning experiences for students into applicable problem-solving efforts, is even more critical today. From a practical standpoint, the notion that students in a language class would all be in the same levels of subjects in other disciplines, i.e., all students taking math statistics or biology at the same time, is not usually feasible at the high school or college level. What the authors point out so well, is that the students themselves can become the purveyors of knowledge based on their subject expertise. What better way to learn than to teach one's peers. Instructors can easily leverage the content-specific knowledge necessary within the students in their classrooms and make them the "experts" in ensuring that the rest of the students are able to integrate the math, science, or social studies aspects into the tasks they face. Finally, having an audience other than the teacher has an extremely empowering effect on students raising their own expectations of themselves. The units described by the authors all have an authentic audience established by the nature of the task itself.

Very valuable to the readers is the authors' efforts to position the development of intercultural citizenship within interdisciplinary units against the backdrop of other instructional tools and approaches such as backward design, essential questions, NCSSFL-ACTFL Language and Intercultural Can-Do Statements. This is important so that instructors understand that this is not an "add-on" to the curriculum but more of an infusion into an already existing framework.

Also important to point out is that while disasters such as Hurricane Maria have taken their toll in countries such as Puerto Rico, we need not embrace these misfortunes as the "fixers" of a situation. It is important to develop in students the idea of empathizer and not sympathizer. This is where the notion of connecting the students themselves into groups that share and then analyze data can be particularly important to increasing students' understanding of the perspectives from other cultures and how they are related to the practices and products of that culture. There are climate crises taking place within the United States currently that international student groups may be able to discuss and make recommendations about that would demonstrate needed changes in American climate policy. The scenarios outlined in the text call for international understanding without one country emerging as all-powerful or all-knowing. This also supports the idea of students as mediators, the important role described by the authors, so that we don't demand judgments on the part of students but instead an openness and acceptance of a variety of opinions and perspectives.

The need for change in the language classroom is clear. Teaching Intercultural Citizenship provides a pathway toward positioning language programs where students experience viable and purposeful learning that has long-lasting impact on their personal and ultimately professional aspirations. We are grateful to Manuela, Fabiana, and Michael for providing such a clear and meaningful roadmap for language educators— helping our learners to "go outside" to discover "what's inside."

— MARTHA G. ABBOTT

Preface

This book is the product of a multi-year collaboration emphasizing use of the theory of Intercultural Communicative Competence and Intercultural Citizenship in practice. 'We' are the authors of this book and the many teachers and students who have helped us. To help 'you,' the reader, better understand our message, here is a brief presentation of the three authors.

Manuela Wagner, an applied linguist, began her career studying how infants and children learn to communicate. Always loving to learn new languages and observe different cultures, she started teaching English in Austria and Germany, followed by Spanish and German in K-12 and at the university in the U.S., while completing her Ph.D. in English with a focus on linguistics at Graz University, Austria. Fostered by her interdisciplinary education (English department in Austria, Max-Planck-Institute for Brain Research in German, and the Harvard Graduate School of Education) her true passion is collaborating with colleagues from different disciplines and in diverse educational settings to investigate difficult questions related to the use of theory and practice. At the University of Connecticut she was hired through the *Teachers for a New Era* grant, which supported the ideals of interdisciplinarity and of conducting research into how to help all students succeed. For her that entails making education relevant for all students and in their lives in the here and now.

Fabiana Cardetti, a research mathematician who became a university professor, loves to help others understand the intricacies, logic, and beauty of mathematics. This passion for teaching was inspired by her father and other extraordinary teachers and colleagues. Soon after joining the faculty at the University of Connecticut, she supported the mathematical education of in-service and pre-service teachers, which prompted a significant change in her research career. While she thoroughly enjoyed tinkering with the theories of geometric control theory, she progressively shifted her focus to fully dedicate to research in mathematics education. She has continued and extended this work in collaboration with colleagues from different disciplines and in active partnership with teachers at different educational levels, aiming to empower all students in their lives and, hopefully, their futures.

Michael (Mike) Byram began as a teacher of languages in an English secondary school, a 'community comprehensive,' and taught French and German to adolescents in the daytime and adults of all ages in the evening. This became the basis for his research on what he originally called *'cultural studies* in foreign language education,' unconsciously using the phrase he had learned from a key intellectual influence, Raymond Williams. He wanted to find ways to consider the cultural dimension of language teaching. In time he created a model of intercultural (communicative) competence in *Teaching and Assessing Intercultural Communicative Competence* (1997), which could be used to systematically plan a cultural dimension and integrate it with language learning. This included the element of 'critical cultural awareness,' the crucial educational feature of the 1997 model, which then became a model of 'Intercultural Citizenship,' introduced in 2008 in *From Foreign Language Education to Education for Intercultural Citizenship.*

We have written this book to engage you in a conversation, which we hope these brief presentations will support. It is part of an ongoing process that began separately in our academic work but then developed into our multi-year collaboration in which we worked at all levels from elementary to higher education in projects involving local and transnational communities, integration of intercultural competence, and a theory of the development of criticality. In the course of this we published the results together (Byram, Conlon Perugini, & Wagner, 2013; Byram, Golubeva, Han, & Wagner, 2017; Wagner, Cardetti, & Byram, 2016; Wagner, Conlon Perugini, & Byram, 2018).

As in all communication, knowing something about each other helps, and we also have a vision of who you, our reader, are. If you decided to pick up this book, you probably already believe that students must be equipped with the knowledge, skills and attitudes to communicate with people of different cultural backgrounds and opinions. You might also say that it is more important than ever to work together and solve problems. We agree, and in the next six chapters we will engage in a conversation with you about language education's central role in preparing students to participate actively and knowledgeably in shaping a more sustainable future.

The work in this book has not only been guided by the collaborations indicated above and in our acknowledgments but also benefited directly from them. Indeed, some of the practical examples we present originated from that work. The people involved are mentioned in the text and acknowledgments, as are those who provided invaluable feedback and input.

We will argue that we must find ways to collaborate across disciplines to ensure that our students apply relevant concepts, skills, and approaches from a variety of disciplines to address some of the complex problems we also expect them to solve "later in life." However, we must make education relevant for our students now, not just for later. In the next chapters we explore ways to facilitate projects in which students apply immediately what they learn in school to a problem they face in their community or in collaboration with peers somewhere else, including other communities in their own country or elsewhere. We suggest how to break through classroom walls and cross borders so our students may realize how interconnected we are locally, nationally and internationally.

We also attempt to eliminate borders between different language educators and between different disciplines. We will emphasize common goals and explore how to reach them. Ultimately, though we recognize the difficulties, we want our learners— and ourselves and our colleagues—to think in borderless ways. In schools and universities, and globally, people have spent a lot of time creating borders and then trying to cross them. When they do not exist, people can concentrate on solving more important problems for the common good.

As we will suggest in this book, this approach requires us all to examine our disciplinary identities as teachers just as it required us, as authors with different national, disciplinary and other identities, to re-examine some of our positions in the course of writing this book. We had to particularly understand and interact with people of a different (disciplinary) culture, which is comparable to any intercultural interaction. Using our intercultural competence as best we could, we endeavored to learn with each other how we could realize our goals. As we had expected, this collaboration continued to open our minds to educational possibilities. It also challenged us to integrate and make sense of differences. In the book we try to show both sides of the coin: how we can simultaneously enrich such interdisciplinary collaborations and address challenges as they occur.

You, our reader, will have similar questions of identification, particularly of disciplinary identity. We do not pretend this is easy, but we hope you will take up the challenge. If you do, please contact us to share your experience.

— MANUELA WAGNER, FABIANA CARDETTI, AND MICHAEL BYRAM
(Storrs, USA and Durham, UK, January, 2019)

Introduction

This is a book for language educators from elementary school to postsecondary education who wish to see and develop new ways to use language education for intercultural communication.

Our ambitious, innovative aims are threefold. First, we want to introduce into language teaching the concept of education for Intercultural Citizenship, to encourage learners of all ages and stages to actively participate in their communities from local to international, bringing to the local an international, intercultural perspective. Second, we want language teachers to teach Intercultural Citizenship through collaboration with educators in other disciplines and to demonstrate to them that collaboration can lead to a fulfilling educational experience for their learners. Finally, we want to persuade (language) educators that they have social responsibilities to educate learners to be intercultural citizens and to accept this as central to their work and professional identities.

Our approach to these three innovations is to engage in a conversation with you about the theoretical and practical tools necessary to integrate into our teaching the knowledge, skills, and attitudes necessary for our students to engage in Intercultural Citizenship from the beginning of their education. We define 'Intercultural Citizenship' as 'being active in one's community—local or beyond the local—and using one's linguistic and intercultural competences to realize and enrich discussions, relationships, and activities with people of varied linguistic and cultural backgrounds.'

This definition shows that language education has immediate as well as long-term effects on our students' lives and roles as conscious, skillful participants and actors in both their immediate school and classroom communities and communities beyond their school walls and national borders. Simultaneously, we consider the philosophy of our approach to have implications for the advocacy of language education in both school and society.

In the 50-year anniversary edition of *Foreign Language Annals,* Moeller & Abbott (2018) ask, "How exactly does one go about making the vision of languages as a core subject for all learners a reality?" (p. 21). We hope that our approach, combined with the advocacy tools and efforts of "Lead with Languages," will provide a rich starting point for a common argument. To that end, this book combines classroom work in languages and other subjects with life outside school. We want to show how language teachers can help students apply the knowledge and skills they have acquired in language learning in other subjects or outside of school. After all, languages are related to all aspects of life, and we want to make sure our students make connections from the very beginning of their language education to help solve the interconnected problems we face today.

In line with our view that, as language teachers, we must eliminate borders, we chose the term 'language education' to refer to what is otherwise also called 'world' or 'foreign' language education. We acknowledge that there might be issues with any term we choose. However, we must note that, for example, Spanish in the U.S. can hardly be called a foreign language.

Overview

In Chapter 1, we present short scenarios that illustrate the outcomes of teaching units created using the theories of Intercultural Competence and Citizenship. The scenarios will show what students can do with their languages, at a given proficiency and education level, by the end of a sequence of lessons focusing on Intercultural Citizenship. The scenarios will also show connections between the theoretical framework and the standards in several disciplines, thereby bridging theory and practice.

You will notice how much education for Intercultural Citizenship is aligned with the goals of education for social justice (Glynn, Wesely, & Wassell, 2014; Osborn, 2006); an example of this will appear in Scenario C in Chapter 1. Wherever appropriate, we will make connections to the *NCSSFL ACTFL Can Do Statements for Intercultural Communication*. In addition, we will share how standards in other subjects, e.g., the Common Core State Standards for Mathematics (CCSSM, 2010), the Next Generation Science Standards (NGSS, 2013), and the National Curriculum for Social Studies (NCSS, 2010), support work in language education and vice versa. This will facilitate the interdisciplinary approach this book introduces and supports.

To a degree we follow a 'backward design' (Wiggins & McTighe, 2005) according to which one starts planning by identifying the desired results. We do this in Chapter 1 using the scenarios as examples of those results. In this chapter and throughout the book, we will invite you to 'Pause to Ponder', before we relay our thinking and approaches, to help you become (more) conscious of your own thinking and reflect on how our approach might work for you.

In Chapter 2, we introduce the theoretical framework on which the units described in the following chapters will be built. This framework comprises theories of Intercultural Competence (Byram, 1997) and Intercultural Citizenship (Byram, 2008). We also show how this framework can be aligned with the *World-Readiness Standards* (National Standards Collaborative Board, 2015) and the assessment of intercultural competence.

Interdisciplinary unit planning is presented in two different ways. First, in Chapter 3, we show how several disciplines can work together in the planning of interdisciplinary learning experiences that meet both Intercultural Citizenship objectives and the objectives specific to each discipline. Second, in Chapter 4, we focus on the planning of learning experiences that support the work across the disciplines with a focus on the language classroom.

More specifically in Chapter 3, we describe the key components necessary for planning lessons and assessments for teaching Intercultural Citizenship across the subjects. We build this chapter around Scenario A from Chapter 1, which addresses the global water crisis, to clarify the interdisciplinary approach with a concrete example. Here we introduce 'interdisciplinarity.' Therefore, throughout, we link theory with practice by providing examples and opportunities for you to reflect on your practice, as well as instructional resources that support planning and assessment of interdisciplinary units like this. As we do so, we ask you to 'Pause to ponder' before we relate our thinking and approaches, to help you become (more) conscious of your own thinking and reflect on how our approach might work for you. As there are fewer details on daily lesson planning in language education, we include some examples at the end of the chapter to prompt you to think about specific ideas for your own teaching before you move to the next chapter, which is much more focused on language teaching.

Emphasizing planning for language teaching, Chapter 4 explores the interdisciplinary connections using Scenario B from Chapter 1 as a concrete illustration, digs deeper into the cross-curricular links, and analyzes how the learning experience supports and enhances all subjects involved. Thus you will see more detailed planning of activities for the language classrooms and the meaningful connections you can make to other disciplines. To illustrate what we mean by working with other disciplines and affecting society in the here and now, we will offer extensions that might happen in other subjects and in the students' first language (L1) outside of the classroom. But we will focus on what the students can do in Intercultural Citizenship in the target language (TL), with scaffolding and recycling of prior knowledge and skills and with pre-prepared, readily available materials online.

Having explained our work in language teaching and how links can be made in practice with other disciplines, in Chapter 5 we address the question you may be asking yourself: "Why do we want to teach languages for interdisciplinary Intercultural Citizenship?" We do so by locating what we advocate for language teachers and their collaborating colleagues in the 'bigger picture' of social and educational change. We also discuss implications for language teachers' identities and the role of language education in the general educational mission and in addressing real-world problems. Here we show that teaching for Intercultural Citizenship also enables language educators to argue the case for language education as a central part of education, not just a peripheral interest for those who think language skills will be useful in their career. At the same time this is the place to clarify the significance of the language teaching profession.

The final chapter returns to practical issues and discusses questions which may have arisen in your mind as you read the previous chapters. The questions are based on our own experience and questions asked by teachers we have worked with. We conclude with a discussion of how we can move forward in our classrooms and as a profession with teaching languages for Intercultural Citizenship using an interdisciplinary approach.

Through these chapters we hope to inspire and encourage you to incorporate Intercultural Citizenship into your teaching practice. Should you take this call for action, we would be happy to hear from you personally or at conferences and in your own publications about what worked and what needs improvement. Only together can we achieve our goal to empower all students through interdisciplinary Intercultural Citizenship education.

What is possible
—IN THE LANGUAGE CLASSROOM AND BEYOND

If foreign-language education is to take learners seriously as legitimate users of the language, scholars and instructors must consider the different ways in which their students could engage with the world beyond the context of classroom (Warner & Dupuy, 2018, p. 124).

We begin with four scenarios describing how learners at the end of a project on Intercultural Citizenship in a language course take their new knowledge into their local community. Beginning at the end helps readers to grasp the innovations in our approach. The bigger picture in which the scenarios and the theory behind them are located is introduced to explain the vision behind this book and the significance of language education in society. Our vision is then linked to recent and current developments in the US and beyond that focus on how intercultural competence in the contemporary world can be systematically taught and assessed.

We intend to offer ways to teach world languages for interdisciplinary Intercultural Citizenship by showing how students can work on real-world issues in the TL and apply what they learn in other subject areas and in their lives, and vice versa. We offer concrete classroom examples that illustrate the theory on which our insights are based, to link theory with practice. The examples are mere suggestions, since all teachers will make up their own minds about how to borrow, modify and develop them. Some will introduce occasional changes in their current practices—for example, a few lessons devoted to a project—while others may completely rethink their language teaching approach. Our intentions will have been realized, whichever response you have.

In this chapter you will read four descriptions of language teaching scenarios show-casing what students can do at the end of a unit involving interdisciplinary teaching. You will be invited to think about commonalities you notice across the scenarios, what strikes you as surprising or new, what you think of this way of language teaching, how you can achieve such outcomes, and how the teacher's role changes in this practice.

We will engage in a dialogue with you, asking you about your perspective and offering our view on these points in the course of the book. Through this and similar conversations with you, we hope to show you that this way of teaching helps you and your students achieve many of the objectives we all seek in (language) education.

You will see that this approach involves students and teachers in thinking about and acting in their community, sometimes 'for real,' sometimes through fictional activities that are nonetheless 'real.' We call this 'teaching for Intercultural Citizenship,' a phrase explained in more detail in Chapter 2 and elaborated on and illustrated throughout the book.

First, we invite you to read these four accounts of the final stages of teaching and learning units developed to teach for Intercultural Citizenship.

Scenario A: A transatlantic middle school project tackling the water crisis[1]

A group of middle-school students is chatting excitedly while preparing to be interviewed for a radio show reporting on innovative educational initiatives. They had collaborated with students in another nation to co-create advertisements that raise awareness of the water crisis and conservation. The primary languages of these groups are different, but they successfully teamed in mixed groups during their world languages classes to understand the water crisis at both local and global levels.

Our middle-school students cannot wait to explain the different contributors to this problem—how they start at their own schools, homes, and communities—and to describe how these are different yet similar to those in the country of their partner group. They will talk about how understanding each other's water consumption customs, significance of water shortage in their respective communities, and present efforts to conserve water in each country, enabled them to better comprehend the global water crisis and seek ways to improve the situation in each place.

The students are eager to talk about different products they have created with their partners in the other country, whose language they are learning. Using the TL, they collaborated on media platforms such as Skype or in online discussion forums sharing, discussing, and investigating the various aspects of the problem and different solutions. They used not only the knowledge of the different countries they had acquired in language lessons but also what they had learned in their social studies, mathematics, and science classes, to look deeply into the problems and generate appropriate solutions.

Students are proud of their products, which include videos, comics, pamphlets, and more! They know that sharing the outcomes of these efforts may show fellow citizens how they can positively affect the world by addressing the water crisis that

> **The students are eager to talk about different products they have created with their partners in the other country, whose language they are learning.**

extends far beyond their own communities. In addition, the students know they may receive feedback from the community that can challenge their ideas and/or extend their understanding of the problem, the solutions, and the community itself.

Scenario B: A high school is reaching out to the local community to discuss preparedness for natural disasters[2]

People are still arriving at the Community Center to attend an event, *Cómo prepararse para un desastre natural: Lecciones del Huracán María* [How to prepare for a natural disaster: Lessons from Hurricane María] the high school students organized. We can hear Spanish and English, and when we enter the room we see notices in both languages. Attendees receive a bilingual program in which the evening's presentations are announced.

In the hallway to the auditorium are posters on topics related to natural disasters, specifically to Hurricane Maria, which occurred in September 2017 in Puerto Rico and Dominica. For example, one poster provides a short history of natural disasters in the U.S. The next presents the statistical analyses and representation of the effects of Hurricane Maria. A third provides information about preparedness for natural disasters in the specific geographical area. Others explain the effects of Hurricane Maria based on interviews with victims, and more.

At 6 p.m. visitors are invited to join student presentations in the main auditorium. After students welcome the audience in English and Spanish, they show a video about a humanitarian crisis caused by a natural disaster (Hurricane Maria). Students then give information in English and Spanish explaining why they decided to plan this public event: so everyone could receive important information about natural disaster preparation. They have also invited community members with direct ties to Hurricane Maria victims to engage in a conversation about ways forward from the disaster, since its effects can still be felt strongly in Puerto Rico and also in their own community.

Finally, they introduce first responders from the local Police and Fire Department, who have agreed to share some important information the students will translate into Spanish.

During the event, students distribute pamphlets with crucial information, e.g., from the Federal Emergency Management Agency (FEMA) in Spanish and English, such as the *Plan familiar de comunicación en caso de emergencia,* [Safety instructions, and telephone numbers in case of emergency].

The poster exhibition will be on display in the community center for another month and will then move to the school.

Scenario C: Students acting as mediators and interpreters for immigrant families[3]

Immigration is a sensitive topic everywhere, and the students in this classroom—11th graders with 3-6 years of Spanish—are now acting out their roles as mediators for immigrant families. Some began their project holding stereotypes and attitudes often found in their society. Their teacher had used a simple questionnaire to establish their views and then discussed stereotypes with them in preparation for their task: to help an immigrant family settle in the United States.

By the end of the project, students had been assigned a (fictional) immigrant family, had become familiar with their situation—the finances they had available, number of children, ambitions, living conditions, English proficiency level—and had helped them to understand the demands their host society had made on them. Students first considered this a matter of translation, interpretation and language, but soon found themselves explaining details of social living—healthcare and insurance, transportation, cost of food and accommodation, choices to be made within the family's budget. At that point their role changed from interpreter/translator to mediator and 'intercultural speaker,' a phrase explained in more detail in Chapter 2.

In the project's final stages, students describe 'their' family, how they had carried out research to help make decisions on budgetary, housing and similar matters, and what they had learned, not only about the immigration experience but also about their own society from a newcomer's perspective. The teacher noticed how difficult this change of perspective was. She reported how students did not generally understand the status of immigrants within the U.S.: 'Do immigrants qualify for Medicaid?' 'How do we get a Green Card?' Students also knew little about average incomes and financial issues for families in the United States. Some groups displayed disbelief at the salaries for 'their' immigrant families, ranging from shock at realizing that people earn so little, to questioning a salary because it seemed too high.

Although this was a classroom project based on fictional scenarios, the teacher was struck by the realism of the experience and the engagement of the students. As someone with many years of teaching experience, the teacher was finally overwhelmed by students' language use: "When students were having conversations in these scenarios, there was a language production level that made me rethink the usual standards."

Scenario D: University students and refugees collaboratively write poems to promote peace[4]

"Breeze, breeze, bring the peace; / War may now forever cease!" postulates a green-bordered poem. Its rhythm is special—almost enchanting—as is the atmosphere at the lakeside on that evening. A team of 22 students from the University of Munich (LMU) and 19 refugees from Munich and surrounding regions has just opened an exhibition that includes 20 poems on the topic of peace. They present the exhibition to a local audience and recite some poems, and soon everybody engages in lively conversation.

Europe has seen heated discussions about how to handle what some call the 'refugee crisis.' These students and refugees participated in an intercultural service-learning project called 'Global Peace Path—Visions, Words and Actions' and collaboratively wrote poems during two full-day workshops. On the first day they exchanged visions of peace, got to know each other, were introduced to writing poetry, and, in mixed groups of two or three people, produced the first version of their poems. On the second day they translated their poems into other languages. The multilingualism of the poems reflects the idea of intercultural dialogue and understanding: German as the local language, English as an international language or *lingua franca*, and a third language serving as a bridge to the cultures of the international participants. While some students admitted holding stereotypes and having reservations against refugees before the first encounter, they later reported how the collaboration helped to build trust: "I think that my image of refugees changed during the workshop. Now I see in them other young people who try to find their way in life."

For the participants, that evening at the lakeside concludes a project that aims at integration and shared commitment to peace. However, they enthusiastically explain that the project has a local as well as global dimension. As follow-up projects are undertaken by other schools and universities worldwide, an expanding Global Peace Path literally emerges. They are ready to make a change and use the foreign language as a vehicle: "Peace is important for every land: / Let's walk together hand in hand!"

■ ■ ■ ■ ■

We intentionally started the book by showing what is possible because (1) it is a good motivation for us all to know what our students can achieve, and (2) it is a sensible practice to know where you want to end up before you plan each step, 'best backwards.'

There are excellent resources that can help you design lessons using backward design. Figure 1.1 represents the different steps taken when a curriculum is planned backwards, based on the stages proposed by Wiggins & McTighe (2005) along with the steps delineated by Glynn, Wesely, & Wassell (2014, p. 26).

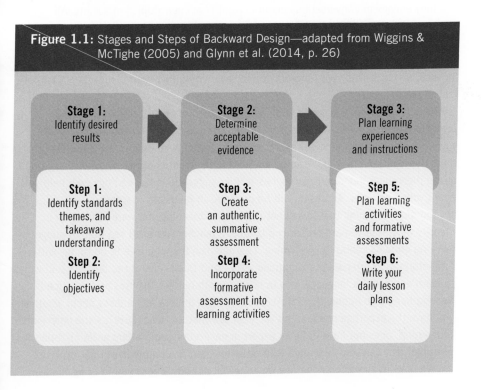

Figure 1.1: Stages and Steps of Backward Design—adapted from Wiggins & McTighe (2005) and Glynn et al. (2014, p. 26)

Stage 1: Identify desired results

Stage 2: Determine acceptable evidence

Stage 3: Plan learning experiences and instructions

Step 1: Identify standards themes, and takeaway understanding

Step 2: Identify objectives

Step 3: Create an authentic, summative assessment

Step 4: Incorporate formative assessment into learning activities

Step 5: Plan learning activities and formative assessments

Step 6: Write your daily lesson plans

Before you continue reading, we ask you to consider the following questions. Our views will be provided in the next section.

Pause to Ponder

1. What do the four scenarios have in common?
2. How well do these scenarios resemble your own classrooms? What is different? What is similar?
3. What appear to be the learning goals the teachers had for the students?
4. How do these compare with your own general goals as an educator, particularly as a language educator?
5. What seems to be the suggested role of language education? Does this resonate with you?

What do these scenarios have in common?

You might have answered that all four scenarios deal with world language education. Students in all four also appear to take their language or TL out into the community to do something with it and with what they learn in school. Moreover, interaction between the students and their real or imagined communities, local or transnational, is apparent. And they engage in conversations about current challenges/topics in society. All four scenarios involve learning something about and from another region or country/countries where the TL is spoken. They might also seem very ambitious and justifiably cause you to ask the question, "How much time would it take to prepare my students for such events?" This could prompt you to say, "While this sounds nice, it is just not realistic in my context."

We aim to convince you that such outcomes are not only desirable but truly possible if planned well. We do not try to plan for you but to provide inspiration for your own planning, through our examples and additional resources, for a number of units that can serve as models to be adapted to different contexts. A solid background in the theoretical framework, as well as further suggestions for readings, will help you adapt your own units. All of this will be provided in following chapters.

You may also think that this is not the kind of teaching you were trained for or identify with, that you are primarily a language teacher. We shall see that language learning remains central to everything. Learners use the language to do things with—find information, prepare presentations, etc.—and this is one of the best ways in which to learn and acquire language, one in keeping with current theories and practice in Second Language Acquisition (SLA). You may nonetheless feel uneasy about whether you have the expertise needed, but we shall see that the teacher is not the only source of learning, does not have to be an expert in environmental matters or immigration for example, and can also cooperate with other teachers to complement their expertise.

We now invite you on a journey we hope will not only cause you to bring the world into your classrooms but also take your students out into the world where they can use their language and their knowledge, attitudes and skills in intercultural affairs—acquired in their language classes of course, but also in their mathematics, social studies, sciences, arts and other classes—to solve problems and build relationships. We are here to break through classroom walls and other barriers that prevent our students from seeing the relevance and importance of language education, and their education in general, for their lives right now and into the future.

How do we envision this transformation of language education?

Language educators plan fantastic activities for their students daily. We have long moved away from *learning about* the TL to learning to actually using it. A well-known approach is to learn language by using it, by learning content in the TL in 'content-based-instruction' (CBI) (Met, 1998) or 'content and language integrated learning' (CLIL) (Coyle, 2007) (See Chapter 5 for a more detailed description of CBI and CLIL.) We have also made progress in assessing our students in what they need to be able to *do* in and with the TL rather than merely on their abstract knowledge *about* it. The term 'can-do' embodies all of this change (as seen in the *World-Readiness Standards for Learning Languages*, National Standards Collaborative Board, 2015; *ACTFL Integrated Performance Assessments*, ACTFL, 2003; *ACTFL Performance Descriptors*, ACTFL, 2015; and *ACTFL Proficiency Guidelines*; ACTFL, 2012).

The last two decades have also seen a push to include not only knowledge *about* culture in language classrooms—the tradition for many decades—but also to teach Intercultural Competence, or the attitudes, skills and knowledge necessary to become intercultural speakers or mediators (Byram & Zarate, 1996, Byram, 1997). A similar independent development has focused on education for social justice in language learning (Glynn, Wesely, & Wassell, 2014; Nieto, 2010; Osborn, 2006).

Furthermore, we want to not only facilitate the development of Intercultural Communicative Competence in our students, hoping they will use it sometime in their future, but also design opportunities with them so they can apply their competence now. In a nutshell, the students in the scenarios introduced above engaged in what Byram (2008) calls Intercultural Citizenship.

Why is it important to engage students in Intercultural Citizenship?

When we consider today's opportunities and challenges, our students' ability to engage in intercultural dialogue at local, national and international levels is essential. We also often lament that students do not seem prepared to address real challenges due to curricula that are still largely based on textbooks, state-mandated tests, and schedules that disregard collaboration (Coffey, 2009).

The *NCSSFL-ACTFL Can-Do Statements,* updated to include this attention to intercultural communication (ACTFL, 2017), are designed to help learners set goals for such communication as they move through the proficiency continuum. Similarly, the Council of Europe (CoE), which comprises the 28 states of the European Union and 19 others, published a guide for all European educators in which they describe what they can do to integrate the knowledge, skills, and attitudes required to engage in intercultural dialogue and democratic culture (Council of Europe, 2018). Furthermore, the Organisation for Economic Co-operation and Development (OECD) has published a plan for assessing 'Global Competence' (youtube.com/watch?v=puYx83MSOgc), an indication of the importance of these issues worldwide.

We will continue to connect to this bigger picture throughout the next chapters and, in Chapter 5, provide more context through current research in Second Language Acquisition and other areas. For now, we maintain that interdisciplinary language education will help our students develop the skills to succeed in today's world. If you prefer to see the bigger picture from the beginning, we recommend reading Chapter 5 now and returning to Chapter 2. If you are more curious about what it is we propose and how it is realized in practice, we suggest reading the chapters in sequence.

Endnotes

[1] We are grateful to Nicole Coleman, Silke Gräfnitz, and Steven LeMay for their work in the collaborative project with Farmington Public Schools, during which the original unit, based primarily in social studies and mathematics, was developed with input from the project's community of practice.

[2] We are grateful to Kyle Evans and Deanne Wallace for their work in the collaborative project with Farmington Public Schools during which the original unit, based primarily in Social Studies and Mathematics, was developed with input from the project's community of practice.

[3] We are grateful to Deanne Wallace and Jocelyn Tamborello-Noble (2018) who initially developed this unit in collaboration with the community of practice we (Mike and Manuela) helped form for a project we published in 2017 (Wagner, Conlon Perugini, & Byram, 2018). A modified and abbreviated version of this unit codesigned and implemented by Andrea Bohling. For more information see Bohling, Wagner, Cardetti, and Byram (2016).

[4] We are grateful to Dr. Petra Rauschert of Ludwig Maximilian Universität, (Munich, Germany) for writing this account of her and her colleague Dr. Claudia Owczarek's work. Further details can be found at: Global Peace Path (n.d.) www.tefl.anglistik.uni-muenchen.de/projects-events/globalpeacepath/index.html

Making it possible
—MODELS AND THEORIES

Education [...] is a process of living and not a preparation for future living. [...] The school must represent present life—life as real and vital to the child as that which he carries on in the home, in the neighbourhood, or on the playground. [...] The moral education centers upon this conception of the school as a mode of social life, that the best and deepest training is precisely that which one gets through having to enter into proper relations with others in a unity of work and thought. (Dewey, 1929, p. 292)

Experience of intercultural (democratic) citizenship can take place in many locations and on many occasions, and individuals may reflect and act together with people of other groups accordingly. The role of education is to anticipate and prepare people for such experience and to promote reflection, analysis and appropriate action. Given the tendency of individuals to remain within the security of their own group and to protect their own self-esteem, there is a significant role for education in preparing them to resist this tendency and meet the challenges involved. (Byram, 2008, p. 187)

This chapter explains the theoretical foundations for the scenarios in Chapter 1 and the explanations of our interdisciplinary approach and proposals for changes in language education in Chapters 3 and 4. Language education has acquired a new and different social purpose as the world has changed through globalization and internationalization. This is apparent in education policies worldwide and in the US. Intercultural Citizenship is the concept we propose to meet the new challenges and opportunities, and provide a firm foundation for language education practice. 'Communicative Language Teaching' can be expanded to enrich the concept of communicative competence with intercultural communicative competence. A model of intercultural communicative competence identifies the skills, knowledge and attitudes which can be taught and learned in language education. Intercultural communicative competence is in turn the foundation for education for Intercultural Citizenship which encompasses concern with social justice, with a questioning attitude to what learners experience in their local, national and international environment, and a concern to make changes for the better. The implications for language educators include: (a) collaboration with teachers of other disciplines, and the example of common ground in mathematics, science, social studies, and language education is discussed; (b) finding appropriate ways of planning and assessing successful learning, both formative and summative; (c) developing techniques for teaching Intercultural Citizenship in the TL. These various aspects of theory are introduced by formulating questions the answers to which provide the preparation for teaching languages for Intercultural Citizenship.

Language teaching in the wider social and human context

The phrase 'communicative language teaching' appeared in the 1970s and was part of the growing emphasis on language teaching and learning for practical purposes, using a language to communicate from the very earliest stages. This 'instrumental' purpose is now complemented by the notion that language teaching and learning has educational and humanistic purposes, too. This is evident for example in the following statement from Norway:

1. Foreign languages are both an educational subject and a humanistic subject. This area of study shall give opportunity for experiences, joy and personal development, at the same time as it opens greater possibilities in the world of work and for study in many language regions.

2. Competences in language and culture shall give the individual the possibility to understand, to 'live into ' and value other cultures' social life and life at work, their modes and conditions of living, their way of thinking, their history, art and literature,

3. The area of study (languages) can also contribute to developing interest and tolerance, develop insight in one's own conditions of life and own identity, and contribute to a joy in reading, creativity, experience and personal development.

4. Good competence in languages will also lay the ground for participation in activities which build democracy beyond country borders and differences in culture. (our (literal) translation—numbering added.)

(Accessed March 2018: www.udir.no/kl06/PSP1-01/Hele/Formaal)

In the first section, we see that language learning has both personal development value and utility as a means of accessing work and study. The second section makes the significance of the cultural dimension of language learning explicit: *language learning should lead to greater understanding of people with other ways of living and thinking.* The third section is an important statement of how language teaching and learning should lead to a better understanding of ourselves, a purpose which has become increasingly part of such documents in the last decade. The final section makes a statement seldom found in such documents, but present at the heart of this book.

This Norwegian document asserts that language learning shall enable students to participate in democratic processes beyond the limits of their own language, culture and country, which is central to our own concept of Intercultural Citizenship. For when we look beyond country borders, it is evident that every day brings a new urgency to come together to recognize and solve problems, such as environmental and humanitarian crises, whose consequences threaten us all if we do not find solutions. This is both a practical/instrumental matter and part of our life as social human beings.

(By the way, we do not want to imply here that the aspirations of this statement are all already realized in practice in Norwegian language teaching. Policy documents nonetheless give us aspirations that help us think in new ways about our practice. This is why we quote this document.)

As a current, vital example of this way of thinking, we see, in Europe, societies facing major questions of social cohesion but suddenly made more visible by the appearance of new groups of refugees, asylum-seekers and voluntary and involuntary migrants. The Council of Europe—with its 48 states stretching from Russia to Greenland, from Finland to Greece—has recognized intercultural dialogue as a basic condition for social cohesion and social justice, and has created a *Reference Framework of Competences for Democratic Culture* (coe.int/en/web/education/competences-for-democratic-culture) in which dialogue and linguistic competences play a crucial part.

❝...language learning shall enable students to participate in democratic processes beyond the limits of their own language, culture and country... ❞

The situation in the United States is in many ways similar, even if the causes are different, and the need to create cohesion through dialogue is the significant background to what we want to say in this book. Despite the common needs, people with different convictions apparently find it harder and harder to communicate with each other and to find a common language both metaphorically and literally (Public Discourse Project, humanities.uconn.edu/about-the-public-discourse-project/). One prerequisite for overcoming this hurdle is to learn to appreciate that people have different beliefs and values and behaviors, and often express them in different languages. As language educators, we are uniquely situated to facilitate students' development of the skills necessary to engage in constructive dialogue and problem-solving with people from a variety of contexts. Here are a few reasons:

1. Intercultural communication is at the heart of (world) language education.
2. Applying content-based language instruction (CBI) approaches, there is no limit regarding the topics that can be covered in our classes and connections that can be made with other subjects and with the real world.
3. As language educators, we also have knowledge that can help us advocate for all language learners (see Additional Reading for more information on the implications for emergent bilinguals).

4. There is a call for and trend toward Action-oriented Approaches (AoA), often using real world tasks to teach languages (Piccardo, 2014).

5. Organizations such as the Council of Europe and ACTFL, as well as Curriculum 21 (Curriculum 21, n.d.), prepare documents that help contextualize such an approach to teaching languages, and other subjects too.

However, to educate our students effectively, we need: (1) clarity about our overall goals, meaning awareness of what it is we want our students to take away from their education; (2) a plan for how we can systematically integrate a theoretical framework; and (3) a way to assess the outcomes.

We want to invite you to pause to ponder what Intercultural Citizenship could mean for you and what your goals are, before we introduce our thinking on these below. Whether you are a novice or an experienced practitioner, we recommend that you take some time to reflect on these foundational questions now, before reading on. After all, you can (and we encourage you to) revisit your responses later; but you will make the most of what we have to offer if you spell out your initial ideas, prior knowledge, and experiences about these questions without the influence of our views. You could start by simply writing a list of concepts and words you associate with 'intercultural' and 'citizenship' separately and together, and then go to the questions in this 'Pause to Ponder.'

Additional Reading

Emergent Bilinguals

In this book, and for our purposes, we use the term emergent bilinguals for students whose L1 is different from the language in the country they live. For example, students in the US who speak Spanish, Chinese, etc. as their L1 are considered emergent bilinguals. The reason we adopted this term is that we want to avoid ignoring the bilingualism of these students. Often there is a view that focuses on deficits rather than seeing this population as a resource.

For example, language educators need to be aware that in the case of emergent bilinguals, it is important to continue to use the home language, in many cases, to ensure academic success, and in all cases to celebrate the whole student and all their identities.

For more information we recommend:

■ García, O. (2009). Emergent Bilinguals and TESOL: What's in a Name? *Tesol Quarterly,* 43(2), 322-326.

Pause TO Ponder

1. In your opinion, what does it mean to be or act as an intercultural citizen? What behaviors are involved? What other characteristics do intercultural citizens have?

2. What is your overarching goal for your students? What do you want them to be able to do at the end of their (language) education?

3. Do you find it difficult to teach Intercultural Citizenship in a systematic way? What challenges do you envision when you think about teaching for a goal beyond just learning the language?

We venture to guess that Intercultural Citizenship plays a role in your teaching. If you responded that you find it difficult to teach Intercultural Citizenship systematically, you are not alone. The good news is that you are also at the right place to find an approach that is doable and successful. Before we share more examples of what this theory looks like in practice, let's take a closer and critical look at the theoretical framework.

Theory of Intercultural Communication in Language Teaching

We must always consider the bigger picture and the social context in which languages are learned and used when we relate to theories. In this book we want to encourage you to think of language teaching and learning as part of that bigger picture, including our social responsibilities as teachers to encourage learners to become involved in the lives of their communities. Language teaching brings an international or intercultural perspective to learners' understanding of themselves and their communities through observation, analysis and understanding of people who speak other languages, whether in their own country or in others. Our experience in working on this basis has shown that students take language learning more seriously; it gives them important knowledge, attitudes and skills and enables them to reflect consciously and critically on their lives and communities. They acquire, as an important part of the educational mission, something they use right now and know they will continue to use.

This way of teaching also requires a change of perspective in terms of how we see ourselves as (language) educators. Rather than viewing ourselves as teachers of a specific language and the related cultures, we advocate for all language learners and for language education for all. The first part means that we see language education as part of the development of a student's identity, and we do not want to forget students who already speak another language. The second part refers to students who might not get the opportunity to learn another language. For all groups of learners, we want to focus on the importance of language education for their development and for becoming active participants in their society, shaping their own future.

Theory of Intercultural Competence and Intercultural Citizenship

The scenarios in Chapter 1 are based on a theoretical framework by which educators may systematically develop the knowledge, skills and attitudes required for Intercultural Citizenship. The framework offers flexibility because of the many connections to other theories and subjects that can be made, but application should be as straightforward as possible. We agree with Toth & Moranski (2018): "Whereas a deeper understanding of principles allows teachers to make needed adaptations to their context, a shallow understanding yields rigid adherence to methodology that is counterproductive, even if its recommendations reflect sound principles." (p. 82) Therefore, at times critical questions will invite you to reflect on the complexity of issues and on the roles of particular contexts.

Before we delve into the specifics, let's discuss concepts related to Intercultural Competence. You must bring to the surface and reflect on the beliefs you have and may not be conscious of, since our goal is to encourage you to adapt the content presented here to your own context.

Pause TO Ponder

1. How do you define 'culture'?
2. In your opinion, what is Intercultural Competence?
3. What must students be able to do to act in an interculturally competent way?

We now address the following questions in turn:
1. What is culture?
2. What is the relationship between language and culture?
3. What is intercultural (communicative) competence?
4. What is Intercultural Citizenship?
5. How does Intercultural Citizenship align with (a) the *World-Readiness Standards*, and (b) the 2017 *NCSSFL-ACTFL Can-Do Statements for Intercultural Communication*?
6. What is the connection between social justice education and (world) language education?
7. How can the work we do in language education support what is done in other subjects, and vice versa?

1. What is culture?

'Culture' is notoriously one of the most complex words in English. It is used in many ways and contexts, and some people recommend we stop using it in our profession because it 'essentializes,' i.e., implies that a country has a single culture that does not change. The word 'culture' is also often misused to refer to any current phenomenon as a culture, e.g., 'the culture of blame' or 'the coffee culture' in our company or country, when all that is being described is what people are doing or thinking in an everyday situation. In one sense this does help, since, as one anthropologist said, "Culture is a verb" (Street, 1993), i.e., it is what groups of people do and, we can add, what they produce as a consequence of what they do.

The groups may be large or small—from a family to a profession to a whole nation—and they share ways of doing things because they share beliefs and values in the life of the group. What they do is visible, and why they do what they do is the underlying set of values and beliefs they hold. Furthermore, groups interact and influence each other, since individuals belong to many groups, and groups living together in a society are often in competition with each other for power and dominance. This means cultures are 'contested' and in constant flux. This has always been so, but has become more evident as change becomes more rapid.

This constant flux means there is some truth in the criticism that talking about 'a culture' is reductive and essentializing. The same could be said about language. A language is in constant flux, as historical dictionaries and grammars show us, and we can all think of words, phrases or ways of saying things that became fashionable and have disappeared, or of others that became fashionable and have become part of ordinary usage; this is one way languages change. Nonetheless, we sometimes choose to teach the language of a specific point in time and a specific group of people, in a simplified way to make it accessible to our learners, especially at the outset. We may then introduce another variety of the language to teach learners that variation and varieties exist. The same applies to 'culture,' and if challenged, we say "for the purposes of our teaching, this is what we mean by 'Spanish language' and 'Spanish culture' "—and then we describe which group at which point in time we are using as our point of reference for the language and culture we teach—or the 'languaculture,' a term we shall return to.

This 'point of reference' does not, however, imply that we believe our learners should imitate native speakers, and we are aware that this is a contentious point. Whether 'the native speaker' should be the model or ideal learners should attempt to imitate in linguistic competence (Davies, 2003) has been much debated, and there are convincing arguments for the view that comparing language learners' language to that of native speakers is not helpful (May, 2013). Whatever decision language teachers may take on linguistic competence, we deem it appropriate for Intercultural Competence (Byram & Wagner, 2018) to use the term 'intercultural speaker' to refer to a language learner who has Intercultural Competence and linguistic competence, whatever the level.

Second, there are good pedagogical reasons for acting *as if* language-and-culture were static. Learners at the beginning of their studies need simplified versions of what they are learning. In language, they learn the regularities and then the exceptions and complexities, although they can be exposed to more complex language along the way. As they become more advanced learners, they can be expected to produce more complex styles and grammatical formations. The same applies to culture, but with one important difference. Because we all tend to seek the comfort and reassurance of our own group—our 'in-group,' be it large or small—we also tend to strengthen its position by denigrating other equivalent 'out-groups.' This leads to stereotypes, i.e., fixed images of other groups, large or small, and to prejudice, i.e., often negative feelings attached to the fixed images. (Something similar may happen with languages, but less often and less obviously.)

In teaching culture, therefore, we must introduce the concepts of 'stereotype' and 'prejudice' and guard against them, from

Additional Reading

For a wide-ranging summary of the research conducted over many years on children's stereotypes, prejudice and perceptions of other countries, we recommend:

- Martyn Barrett (2007) *Children's Knowledge, Beliefs and Feelings About Nations and National Groups* (New York: Psychology Press—Taylor and Francis Group).

Here you will find analyses of the effects of schooling, the role of parents and the media and the many other factors that affect children's and young people's perceptions.

the beginning. The terms themselves need not be used immediately—just as sometimes we decide not to use grammatical terms until later in the learning process—but even young learners acquire stereotypes and prejudices, or have them already before they begin learning a language. Language teachers must constantly remind learners that what they are learning is a simplified version of reality, and that, for example, they would be offended if people of other countries had stereotypes and prejudices about them. We need to teach them not to form premature judgments and to stay open-minded to ambiguities and to deviations from the norm.

What this means in our experience is that students need not have a 'neat' idea of culture. They might need some 'organization of shared meanings' in their minds so they may understand what culture means and how it can be different. However, Manuela Wagner always mentions to her students that her intention is to confuse them. If students become observers (ethnographers) and ask more questions than they find answers, she is fine with it, as a healthy dose of doubt nurtures their curiosity and intellectual humility. The same is true for younger learners. As long as students can grasp that culture is dynamic, we are indeed doing our jobs as educators.

In the *World-Readiness Standards for Learning Language* and in the *NCSSFL-ACTFL Can-Do Statements for Intercultural Communication,* we now have the means to adapt a systematic, pedagogically well-founded approach to culture. In the Standards document, culture is defined in terms of Perspectives (the beliefs and values of a group), Practices (what people in groups do) and Products (the results, both tangible and intangible, of what they do and the perspectives that underpin their doings). In the 'Can-Do' document, cultural learning is linked to the three modes of communication—Interpretive, Interpersonal, and Presentational—and also to 'Intercultural Communication' in which learners' abilities to 'Investigate Products and Practices to Understand Cultural Perspectives' and to 'Interact with Others in and from Another Culture,' are clearly described across proficiency levels and illustrated with performance indicators, as we shall see in more detail below. All of this offers us a means of organizing our teaching and assessment in a systematic way for cultural learning the way we already had for language learning. In the next chapter, we will explain in more detail how this is done, and done in the TL.

The use of the target language (TL)

The use of the TL is important for students to learn the language in question. This notion is supported by ACTFL (2012), which recommends 90% use of the TL in world language classrooms. In their position statement you will find a list of strategies for successful use of the TL:

1. to provide comprehensible input directed toward communicative goals;
2. to make meaning clear through body language, gestures, and visual support;
3. to conduct comprehension checks to ensure understanding;

4. to negotiate meaning with students and encourage negotiation among them;
5. to elicit talk that increases in fluency, accuracy, and complexity over time;
6. to encourage self-expression and spontaneous use of language;
7. to teach students strategies for requesting clarification and assistance when faced with comprehension difficulties; and
8. to offer feedback to nurture students' ability to interact orally in the TL.

As the document explains, ACTFL's recommendation is based on research investigating comprehensible input (Krashen, 1982), input and interaction (Long, 1981), and output (Swain, 1995) in SLA. Although it makes sense that we learn a language by teaching in the TL, it is not always easy for educators to put this recommendation in practice. Research has also shown that, especially in beginning language courses, educators find it hard to teach concepts such as intercultural competence in the TL (Garrett-Rucks, 2013). We could add a number of anecdotes to this conversation in which language educators shared their concerns with us that, while they fully support teaching languages for Intercultural Citizenship, this is surely only possible when students have already acquired some proficiency in the TL. Our response is: we understand that it can be challenging to learn and express cognitively demanding content in the TL, but it is important and possible to do so.

Additional Reading

Target Language

Below we provide some references which have been helpful in our planning. We find that discussion forums (e.g., on Twitter, Facebook, or other social media) can also offer solid sources to support the scaffolding of content in the TL.

■ ACTFL (2012). *Use of target language in language learning.* Available at: https://www.actfl.org/guiding-principles/use-target-language-language-learning.

■ Clementi, D., & Terrill, L. (2017). *The keys to planning for learning: Effective curriculum, unit, and lesson design.* (second edition). Alexandria, VA: American Council on the Teaching of Foreign Languages.

■ Sandrock, P. (2010). *The keys to assessing language performance: Teacher's manual.* Alexandria, VA: American Council on the Teaching of Foreign Languages.

■ Shrum, J. L., Glisan, E. W. (2015). *Teacher's handbook, contextualized language instruction.* Cengage Learning.

■ VanPatten, B. (2017). *While we're on the topic: BVP on language, acquisition, and classroom practice.* Alexandria, VA: American Council on the Teaching of Foreign Languages.

To summarize, we can say that, for the purposes of language teaching, "culture is what a group of people who speak a particular language do ('practices'), why they do what they do ('perspectives'), and what they produce in doing ('products')." We then need to teach our students how to observe, investigate and analyze through comparison with their own group's 'doings,' so they can interact successfully, positively and respectfully with people of another group.

2. What is the relationship between language and culture?

A stimulating term with which to begin the response to this question is 'languaculture,' a word invented by anthropologists but also useful to language teachers. It implies that language and culture are inseparable, a view many language teachers take. Before we accept that view, however, we must examine the relationship between language and culture in more detail.

Risager (2006) analyzes the relationship of language and culture—the 'language-culture nexus'—from three perspectives, summarized below:

1. 'Linguistic practice,' or the sociological perspective, where language and culture are separable (people use the same language in different contexts to refer to and express different contents), is most evident in the use of English in many different countries, but is also found in other languages, such as Spanish.

2. 'Linguistic resources,' or the psychological perspective, where, in the life of the individual person, language and culture or, better, languacultural experience, are inseparable for that individual and are ultimately unique to the individual.

3. 'Linguistic system,' or the theoretical linguistics perspective, where we might analyze and describe the grammar of a language but find no necessary relationship to a cultural context (pp. 110-135).

As linguists, we may be interested in language itself—in its forms, regularities and exceptions. As language teachers, we sometimes isolate the language from context to focus on forms of language. But then we need to put it back into the context we are creating for our learners so it becomes a languacultural experience. As language learners, languacultural experience is our ultimate goal in another language, as in our first or second languages.

Hoffmann (1989) describes the relationship in her autobiography. Neither a linguist nor a language teacher, she describes her languacultural experience in brilliant, non-technical language. Below is her account of her first experience of learning English, having emigrated from Poland to Canada about the age of 12:

> The words I learn now don't stand for things in the same unquestioned way they did in my native tongue. 'River' in Polish was a vital sound, energized with the sense of riverhood, of my rivers, of my being immersed in rivers. 'River' in English is cold—a word without an aura. It has no accumulated associations for me, and it does not give off the radiating haze of connotation. It does not evoke. (Hoffman, 1989, p. 106)

At this point in her life, only Polish is a languaculture. But as she gradually learns and experiences English, it, too, becomes a languaculture for her—one she can then compare with her Polish languaculture.

As language teachers, we need to be aware of all three perspectives Risager identifies. But it is the second that we hope to provide for our learners, to help them to acquire a new languaculture and overcome the difficulties they will inevitably have in the earliest stage, as Hoffmann did.

3. What is Intercultural (Communicative) Competence?

Although the introduction of 'communicative language teaching' prompted language teachers to pay attention to socially appropriate use of language as well as correct grammatical formulation, this was above all a matter of 'politeness' and learning to imitate (part of) the use of a language by native speakers. Intercultural Competence is not the same; not all native speakers have Intercultural Competence, which is an ability to see and use relationships between languacultures.

Intercultural Competence has been seriously discussed in relation to foreign-language education only since the 1990s. Similar concepts (e.g., cultural sensitivity, cultural competence, transcultural or cross-cultural competence) have been studied, in some cases for much longer, in other disciplines (psychology, linguistics, business studies, anthropology, and communication studies, just to name a few). The approaches taken have helped our understanding of what it means to engage in dialogue with people from different backgrounds. For the purpose of this chapter we will focus on one approach developed for foreign-language education but since used in other subjects and contexts.

In the 1990s, Byram (1997) formulated a description of Intercultural Communicative Competence which, in contrast to a number of others, was developed to help language teachers to formulate objectives for teaching and assessment. Building on work first done with Zarate to support the development of the *Common European Framework of Reference for Languages* (Council of Europe, 2001) and stimulated by cooperation with colleagues at the National Foreign Language Center in Washington, D.C., he provided a 'model' of Intercultural Competence that lists knowledge, attitudes and skills important in intercultural communication and teachable in the language classroom. The model has subsequently been used in other contexts, e.g., to help mathematics teachers formulate some of their teaching objectives focused on helping learners to articulate and communicate their mathematical knowledge and

> ❛❛ Intercultural Competence is not the same as politeness; not all native speakers have Intercultural Competence, which is an ability to see and use relationships between languacultures. ❜❜

understanding (Cardetti, Wagner, Byram, 2018; Wagner, Cardetti, Byram, 2016). The model defines five dimensions of Intercultural Competence as follows:

1. *Knowledge:* Knowledge of social groups and their products and practices in one's own and in one's interlocutor's country or region, and of the general processes of societal and individual interaction.
2. *Skills of interpreting and relating:* Ability to interpret a document or event from another culture, to explain it and relate it to documents or events from one's own culture.
3. *Skills of discovery and interaction:* Ability to acquire new knowledge of a culture and cultural practices, and ability to operate knowledge, attitudes and skills under the constraints of real-time communication and interaction.
4. *Attitudes:* Curiosity and openness, readiness to suspend disbelief about other cultures and belief about one's own culture.
5. *Critical cultural awareness:* Ability to evaluate perspectives, practices and products in one's own and other cultures and countries, both critically and on the basis of explicit criteria (Fig. 2.1)

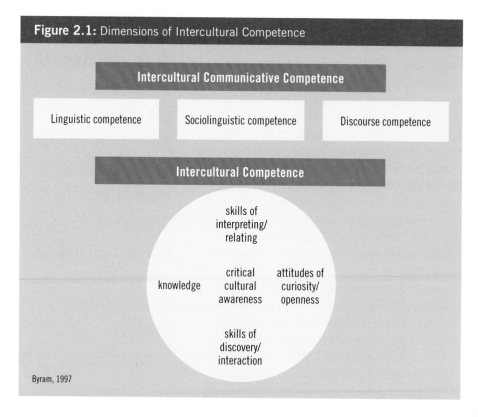

Figure 2.1: Dimensions of Intercultural Competence

Intercultural Communicative Competence

Linguistic competence   Sociolinguistic competence   Discourse competence

Intercultural Competence

skills of interpreting/ relating

knowledge   critical cultural awareness   attitudes of curiosity/ openness

skills of discovery/ interaction

Byram, 1997

Notice that the whole figure is a model of Intercultural *Communicative* Competence, because it includes both Intercultural Competence and the language competences. For, when combined with language competences (linguistic, sociolinguistic, discourse), which are a natural and fundamental part of language education, the model describes

'Intercultural Communicative Competence.' On the other hand, the five elements of 'Intercultural Competence' are important in any intercultural communication—i.e., communication among people of different cultural backgrounds—even when the people involved are speaking the same language and live in the same country.

In the examples throughout this book we illustrate how language educators can collaborate with colleagues in other disciplines to develop the five dimensions of students' Intercultural Competence in a variety of contexts and subjects. Language education, however, focuses on developing Intercultural Competence in combination with the language competences to practice intercultural communication in the TL, hence foster Intercultural *Communicative* Competence.

To summarize the crucial elements of teaching for Intercultural Competence in language teaching, here is a table of characteristics and comments:

Characteristics of intercultural approach to language teaching	Comments
a focus on the learners acquiring knowledge and understanding (not just information) about people who speak the TL (not necessarily only native speakers) and a corresponding knowledge about learners themselves	This focus does not replace but complements attention to language in itself and its structures, functions and semantics, the third kind of language-culture nexus.
the encouragement and planned development of attitudes of curiosity and critical questioning	This replaces the focus on 'tolerance' which is to be found in many (policy and curriculum) statements about the aims of language teaching, and introduces the concepts of critical cultural awareness and social justice.
the teaching and learning of skills of enquiry from which knowledge about self and others evolves, and the skills of comparison as the juxtaposition from which understanding is derived	This creates a 'mutual gaze' in which we see ourselves as others see us, to complement the gaze on others which has been the exclusive direction in language teaching so far.

'Critical cultural awareness' is at the center of Intercultural Competence in this model. This is crucial, as it makes the model different from many others that focus only on skills, attitudes and knowledge. It is the element that emphasizes critical understanding, which is fundamental to good education and is related to teaching languages for social justice (Osborn, 2006). Critical cultural awareness is the element of Intercultural Competence that is developed further in the concept of 'Intercultural Citizenship.'

Related approaches to criticality, which may be interesting, especially to teachers in higher education, have been put forward by various theorists and philosophers of education. Barnett, in his book with the telling title *Higher Education—A Critical Business* (1997), identifies three different domains and four increasingly complex levels of criticality in higher education:

Three Domains of Criticality

1. *Propositions, Ideas And Theories*—i.e., what learners learn about the world (in formal education what they learn in their 'subjects');
2. *The Internal World*, that is oneself, a form of critical thought demonstrated in critical self-reflection—i.e., what learners think about themselves as individuals; and
3. *The External World*, a form of critical thought demonstrated in critical action—i.e., what learners do as a result of their thinking and learning.

Four Levels of Criticality

Critical Skills – Reflexivity – Refashioning Of Traditions – Transformatory Critique

1. At the first level, the emphasis is on *skills* of learning how to be critical (which does not mean being negative or attacking something/somebody, but evaluating positive and negative).
2. At the second level, the skills are *applied* to the knowledge learners have acquired, to their own selves and to the world.
3. At the third level, the criticality leads to *change* in the sense of modification of what has so far been accepted as 'common sense' in knowledge, in oneself, in what we do in the world.
4. At the fourth level, the change is more *radical*. Here, change is not just modification of what is 'common sense' or 'taken for granted' but is overturning this and developing something new.

In projects we have been involved in, teachers across all grade levels (K-20) have made Barnett a foundation for their work (Byram, Golubeva, Han, & Wagner, 2017). A second perspective is offered by colleagues applying critical pedagogy and social justice to language teaching (Glynn, Wesely, & Wassell, 2014; Nieto, 2009; Osborn, 2006). In teaching for social justice as well as Intercultural Citizenship, the teachers must reflect deeply on their own perceptions, values, and beliefs as well as on those underlying assumptions fostered through the curriculum and teaching materials. Both approaches also help students engage in critical reflections on themselves and their roles in the world.

Mediation and the Mediator

People who have some degree of intercultural communicative competence have, first, the skills, attitudes and knowledge with which to explore and understand unfamiliar cultures for themselves. They also have the capacity to help others without such competence to engage with an unfamiliar culture and, in particular, to engage in an intercultural encounter. For example, students can act as mediators for other members of their families when they have guests who have different ways of doing things and reasons for doing so, since 'culture is a verb.' In the scenarios in Chapter 1, we also saw students mediating knowledge of other countries and cultures to members of their local communities.

Mediation is therefore a term now used in descriptions of the objectives of language teaching and is not to be confused with other uses in contexts of (e.g., industrial) strife or (e.g., military) conflict. In the latter cases, the mediator attempts to resolve a dispute to the satisfaction of all parties by remaining neutral and making evident to the disputants where they have common ground and a means of taking action together. In language teaching, the focus is on the competences needed to overcome problems experienced as a consequence of two or more parties not speaking the same language and following the same culture. The emphasis is on the language competences of the mediator, and on their critical understanding of the cultures salient in an interaction.

Additional Reading

Mediation

The following is a useful starting point for more reading on this:

- Zarate, G., Gohard-Radenkovic, A., Lussier, D. & Penz, H. (Eds.) (2004) *Cultural mediation in language learning and teaching*, Kapfenberg: Council of Europe Publishing.

https://www.ecml.at/tabid/277/PublicationID/42/Default.aspx

Mediation is also developed and descriptors provided in the Common European Framework for Languages Companion Volume with New Descriptors (Council of Europe, 2018) https://www.coe.int/en/web/common-european-framework-reference-languages

4. What is Intercultural Citizenship?

In the initial discussion of Intercultural Citizenship, Byram (2008) observed much convergence between teaching the competences of the good citizen and teaching Intercultural Competence. There are also divergences. In citizenship education, the (sometimes implicit, sometimes explicit) purpose is to develop good citizens of the country in which the students live, a *national* perspective. In language education, the perspective is *international*; students are encouraged to look beyond the limits of their own countries and to think about their relationships with others in other countries or with others in their own communities. Citizenship education strongly emphasizes students using their citizenship competences 'in the here and now' to take some action in their own community, to improve in some (often small) way the life of the community. This is well articulated in the *U.S. National Standards for Civics and Government* (Center for Civic Education, 2014):

> The goal of education in civics and government is informed, responsible participation in political life by competent citizens committed to the fundamental values and principles of American constitutional democracy. Their effective, responsible participation requires the acquisition of a body of knowledge and of intellectual and participatory skills. [...] capacity to participate in the political process and contribute to the healthy functioning of the political system and improvement of society (http://www.civiced.org/standards?page=stds_toc_intro—accessed October 2018)

This focus on action in the here and now does not usually exist in language education. Intercultural Citizenship combines the two perspectives to create in students an interest in, and the competences necessary for, taking action in their community, which is often but not always influenced by an international perspective. It is also a humanistic perspective, as articulated in the Norwegian document cited earlier and in the practices of human rights education. This is well formulated in the phrase 'learning to live together,' the most important of the four pillars of education described in the UNESCO report *Learning: the treasure within* (UNESCO, 1996):

> [...] learning to live together, by developing an understanding of others and their history, traditions and spiritual values and, on this basis, creating a new spirit which, guided by recognition of our growing interdependence and a common analysis of the risks and challenges of the future, would induce people to implement common projects or to manage the inevitable conflicts in an intelligent and peaceful way (p. 20).

Significant characteristics of Intercultural Citizenship include:

- a concern about social justice and a belief in the values of humanistic thought and action;
- a readiness to encourage a questioning attitude that recognizes the positive and negative in a social group's beliefs, values and behaviors when evaluated against humanistic standards;
- a willingness to promote social action in the world and the creation of identification with others beyond the limits of national boundaries.

In practice this might involve:

- inclusion of students in decisions about the focus of their learning;
- learning activities that lead to engagement with people from outside the classroom;
- taking decisions to participate in community life outside the classroom by drawing on competences acquired within the classroom.

Intercultural Citizenship theory and practice has also been usefully combined with the theory and practice of 'Intercultural Service-Learning' as illustrated in Scenario D in Chapter 1. There are many similarities between these theories, and the idea of service-learning is well developed in American educational systems.

Additional Reading

Intercultural Citizenship And Service-Learning

- Byram, M. (2008) *From Foreign Language Education to Education for Intercultural Citizenship.* Bristol: Multilingual Matters.
- Byram, M., Golubeva, I., Han H. and Wagner, M. (eds.) (2017) *From Principles to Practice in Education for Intercultural Citizenship.* Bristol: Multilingual Matters

For a discussion of how Intercultural Citizenship and Intercultural Service-Learning enrich each other in theory and in practice, see:

- Rauschert, P. & Byram, M. (2018) Service-Learning and Intercultural Citizenship in Foreign-Language Education, *Cambridge Journal of Education,* 48 (3) 353-369 DOI: 10.1080/0305764X.2017.1337722
- Pak, C. S. (2010). Toward a development of global communities within: Service-learning projects in a business Spanish course. *Global Business Languages,* 5(1), 6.
- Pak, C. S. (2013). Service-learning for students of intermediate Spanish: Examining multiple roles of foreign language study. *MultiTasks, MultiSkills, MultiConnections,* 103.

Pause TO Ponder

Please think again about the scenarios in Chapter 1.

1. What characteristics of Intercultural Citizenship were evident in what the students were doing?

2. In what ways were they 'learning to live together' and to take action in their communities?

3. Do you see an influence by international perspectives? How?

We suggest you keep your answers to these questions in mind. Our own answers will become evident as you read further in the book.

5. How does Intercultural Citizenship align with (a) the *World-Readiness Standards*, and (b) the *2017 NCSSFL-ACTFL Can-Do Statements for Intercultural Communication?*

From the two quotes below, you will see immediately that the concepts presented in this book align with the World-Readiness Standards for Learning Languages (National Standards Collaborative Board, 2015) as well as with the NCSSFL-ACTFL Can-Do Statements for Intercultural Communication (2017).

> The five "C" goal areas (Communication, Cultures, Connections, Comparisons, and Communities) stress the application of learning a language beyond the instructional setting. The goal is to prepare learners to apply the skills and understandings measured by the Standards, to bring a global competence to their future careers and experiences (ACTFL, 2015, p. 2, https://www.actfl.org/sites/default/files/publications/standards/World-ReadinessStandardsfor LearningLanguages.pdf).

> The introductory document to the *NCSSFL-ACTFL Can-Do Statements for Intercultural Communication* (2017) defines Intercultural Communicative Competence as: the ability to interact effectively and appropriately with people from other language and cultural backgrounds. ICC develops as the result of a process of intentional goal-setting and self- reflection around language and culture and involves attitudinal changes toward one's own and other cultures. Intercultural Communicative Competence is essential for establishing effective, positive relationships across cultural boundaries, required in a global society (p. 5).

Pause TO Ponder

1. When you think about the main points of the theoretical framework of Intercultural Citizenship, how do the two quotes above, in addition to what you know about the *World-Readiness Standards* and the *NCSSFL-ACTFL Can-Do Statements for Intercultural Communication,* support our intention to teach languages for Intercultural Citizenship and to help our students engage in meaningful dialogue with people from different backgrounds and opinions?
2. Investigate www.actfl.org and find the *World-Readiness Standards and the NCSSFL-ACTFL Can-Do Statements for Intercultural Communication.* The following categories could be helpful: *Theoretical background, Tools for teachers, Tools for students, Assessments, Resources.*

The main point is that many resources can help you create your philosophy for teaching languages for intercultural communication and citizenship, and provide tools for you and your students. For example, combining our framework with proficiency-based teaching through the three modes of communication facilitates lesson planning and assessments and provides a framework that has been tried and tested. Our activities are all based on the *World-Readiness Standards,* and at times we refer to the *NCSS-FL-ACTFL Can-Do Statements for Intercultural Communication.*

NCSSFL-ACTFL and Intercultural Communicative Competence

Intercultural communication is based on Intercultural Communicative Competence defined, for the purposes of the NCSSFL-ACTFL document, as 'the ability to interact effectively and appropriately with people from other language and cultural backgrounds,' and is described as 'essential for establishing effective, positive relationships across cultural boundaries, required in a global society.' Intercultural communication consists of the ability to 'investigate' and 'interact,' which correspond to one dimension—'skills of discovery and interaction'—of the model we use in this book. Each of these has a 'benchmark' describing the competence involved and a 'performance indicator,' i.e., an observable behavior that manifests the benchmark competence. Examples are then provided, which can be amended to relate to specific languages and cultures.

A comparison of the 'Intermediate' level and the level immediately above it, 'Advanced,' illustrates how the progression is conceived and formulated. Consider, for example, the Intermediate 'Investigate' benchmark with the corresponding one at 'Advanced' level:

- In my own and other cultures I can make comparisons between products and practices to help me understand perspectives.

  AND

- In my own and other cultures I can explain some diversity among products and practices and how it relates to perspectives.

There is a progression from comparison to explanation, from establishing the existence of diversity to explaining it in terms of 'perspectives,' i.e., a group's beliefs and values. The Intermediate 'Interact' benchmark may then be compared with the one at 'Advanced' level:

- I can interact at a functional level in some familiar contexts.

  AND

- I can interact at a competent level in familiar and some unfamiliar contexts.

Here is a distinction between 'functional' and 'competent' interaction and between 'familiar' and 'familiar and some unfamiliar.' The second distinction is easy enough to make, but the first is best understood by looking at examples. In one example, the key phrase at 'Intermediate' level is 'learned behaviors':

- I can use learned behaviors when visiting someone's home or business and notice when I make a cultural mistake.

In contrast, in an example from 'Advanced' level, the key word is 'adjust':

- I can adjust my personal space and body language accordingly when interacting with others in a business, school or work environment.

In another example, the key word is 'manage.' Such words indicate competence, the ability to develop new linguistic and behavioral responses, rather than simply recall and repeat what has been learned in a formulaic way.

A full account of the 'can-do' statements can be found at: https://www.actfl.org/publications/guidelines-and-manuals/ncssfl-actfl-can-do-statements, and in the box below are extracts which we have drawn on in this brief discussion of progression.

Intermediate

Intermediate 'Investigate' benchmark: In my own and other cultures I can make comparisons between products and practices to help me understand perspectives.

Performance indicator: In my own and other cultures I can compare products related to everyday life and personal interests or studies.

Performance indicator: In my own and other cultures I can compare practices related to everyday life and personal interests or studies.

Intermediate 'Interact' benchmark: I can interact at a functional level in some familiar contexts.

Performance indicator: I can converse with peers from the target culture in familiar situations at school, work, or play, and show interest in basic cultural similarities and differences.

Performance indicator: I can recognize that significant differences in behaviors exist among cultures, use appropriate learned behaviors, and avoid major social blunders.

[Some] Examples: Linking Investigation and Interaction:

Investigate: In my own and other cultures I can compare how and why houses, buildings, and towns affect lifestyles.

Interact: I can use learned behaviors when visiting someone's home or business, and I can notice when I make a cultural mistake.

Investigate: In my own and other cultures I can compare events and beliefs that drive the creation of a monument or the popularity of a landmark.

Interact: I can show respect when visiting a historical site by dressing appropriately, adjusting the volume of my voice, and acting with consideration for others.

Investigate: In my own and other cultures I can compare school/learning environments and curricula to determine what is valued.

Interact: I can meet with an advisor in the target culture to select courses that match my preferences and academic goals.

Advanced

Advanced 'Investigate' benchmark: In my own and other cultures I can explain some diversity among products and practices and how it relates to perspectives.

Performance indicator: In my own and other cultures I can explain how a variety of products of public and personal interest are related to perspectives.

Performance indicator: In my own and other cultures I can explain how a variety of practices within familiar and social situations are related to perspectives.

Advanced 'Interact' benchmark: I can interact at a competent level in familiar and some unfamiliar contexts.

Performance indicator: I can converse comfortably with others from the target culture in familiar and some unfamiliar situations and show some understanding of cultural differences.

Performance indicator: I can demonstrate awareness of subtle differences among cultural behaviors and adjust my behavior accordingly in familiar and some unfamiliar situations.

[Some] Examples: Linking Investigation and Interaction:

Investigate: In my own and other cultures I can describe the cultural influences on the designs of houses, buildings and towns.

Interact: I can adjust my personal space and body language accordingly when interacting with others in a business, school or work environment.

Investigate: In my own and other cultures I can describe and explain how landmarks and monuments contribute to national identity.

Interact: I can manage my non-verbal reactions and personal space when in a crowded environment such as standing in line.

Investigate: In my own and other cultures I can explain how beliefs and values are reflected in educational testing, ceremonies and certificates.

Interact: I can complete the requirements of an undergraduate course in the target culture.

Assessment of Intercultural Competence is facilitated by the Can-Do statements, just as similar statements are used in the assessment of linguistic competence. Assessment falls broadly into two categories—formative and summative—and Can-Do statements may be used in both. When used in formative assessment, Can-Do statements help learners to analyze their current competence and then plan, alone or with assistance, how they want to progress to the next level.

Learners and educators can track progress by keeping a record, for example, in a portfolio of their work which illustrates their activities at a specific level. This is similar to the formative assessment of linguistic competence and is especially important in intercultural competence, because learners may not immediately see the relevance and significance of intercultural competence as they do of linguistic competence. 'The language class is where one learns to speak a language' seems obvious enough, but learners need to understand that 'speaking a language' is successful only if they also have intercultural competence.

Summative assessment is important, both for learners as they reflect on their progress over a course of study and as part of the certification of success in learning by which learners can progress to the next stage of education or to prove their competence to employers and others in the wider society. Employers and others also assume that learning a language is learning to 'speak,' and language educators and learners themselves must evince intercultural competence as well as linguistic proficiency so others also understand its significance. Summative assessment evincing what learners 'can do' in intercultural encounters is crucial in this. The approaches to assessment we shall illustrate in later chapters are part of the means of making intercultural competence part of the thinking of people outside language education and outside educational institutions.

6. What is the connection between social justice education and (world) language education?

Researchers and practitioners alike have argued for critical approaches to education in general and to world language education in particular. Here we provide a short introduction to social justice education in language education, which we hope will lead you to investigate this topic further.

In *Teaching World Languages for Social Justice,* Osborn (2006) suggests social justice education as a "framework for inquiry, not a pedagogical end in itself" (p. 29), emphasizing adjustment to the different contexts in which this framework is used. More specifically, renowned social justice education researcher and educator Nieto (2010) describes social justice education as a "philosophy, an approach, and actions that embody treating all people with fairness, respect, dignity, and generosity" (p. 46). This resonates with the practitioner's perspective of Richard de Meji, a world language teacher and social justice educator from Hartford, Connecticut, cited in Glynn, Wesely & Wassell's (2014) *Worlds and Actions: Teaching Languages Through the Lens of Social Justice:* "For me, social justice is the enabling of people to realize their full potential in their society, as a result of experiencing equitable access to liberties, rights and resources (legal, civic, health, social, financial, learning/academic, political, technological, etc.) in their society" (p. 2).

Even these few descriptions reveal key connections between social justice education and teaching (languages) for Intercultural Citizenship. Nieto (2010) proposes similar approaches under the umbrella term of diversity education: "Multicultural education, intercultural education, nonracial education, antiracist education, culturally responsive pedagogy, ethnic studies, peace studies, global education, social justice education, bilingual education, mother tongue education, integration—these and more are the terms used to describe different aspects of diversity education around the world" (p. 1). Glynn, Wesely, & Wassell (2014) advocate social justice education as an approach that benefits all students and teachers: "The world language classroom is uniquely suited to challenge, confront, and disrupt misconceptions, untruths, and stereotypes that lead to structural inequality and discrimination based on social and human differences" (p. 3), providing yet another connection to teaching for Intercultural Citizenship. Additionally, Reagan & Osborn (2002) identify the role of world language education in developing students' language and social awareness, in particular to counter oppression.

A prerequisite for teachers to teach for social justice is to understand that teaching is inherently political (c.f., Freire, 1993; Osborn, 2006, Reagan & Osborn, 2002). Nieto (2010) provides a description of attributes successful social justice educators have:

> The most successful teachers with whom I have had the privilege to work are skilled in their pedagogy, well versed in their subject matter, and consciously political in the sense that they know their work makes a difference. Consequently, they embody particular behaviours and attitudes that help them both teach and reach their students, while at the same time they challenge inequities both in their schools and, more broadly, in their societies. (p. 42)

Furthermore, Osborn (2006) describes teaching world languages for social justice as "involving inquiry *with* (not about or on) the students and the community, which may be focused on problems" and as being "connected to other, broader social movements" (p. 33). Social justice education thus helps students think about how they can make a difference in their local and global communities.

Additional Reading

Education For Social Justice

- Freire, P. (1993). *Pedagogy of the Oppressed.* 1968. New York: Continuum.

- Glynn, C., Wesely, P., & Wassell, B. (2014). *Words and Actions: Teaching Languages through the Lens of Social Justice.* Alexandria, VA: American Council on the Teaching of Foreign Languages.

- Nieto, S. (2002). *Language, Culture, and Teaching: Critical perspectives.* Mahwah, NJ: Lawrence Erlbaum.

- Osborn, T. A. (2006). *Teaching World Languages for Social Justice: A Sourcebook of Principles and Practices.* Mahwah, NJ: Lawrence Erlbaum.

- Reagan, T. G., & Osborn, T. A. (2002). *The Foreign Language Educator in Society: Toward a Critical Pedagogy.* New York: Routledge.

7. How can the work we do in language education support what is done in other subjects, and vice versa?

Language education is well-positioned to support and be supported by learning in other subject areas, especially now that new research on teaching and learning has prompted a significant shift in such subject areas as mathematics, science, and social studies; over the past few years these subjects have embarked on an overhaul of their state standards with a new focus on what students need to learn and how it must be taught. This new approach enables us to work collaboratively with language teachers to foster students' communication and problem-solving skills across subjects.

Specifically, the Common Core State Standards Initiative (CCSSM, 2010) high-lighted the importance of engaging students at all school levels in some neglected key mathematical practices to succeed in mathematics. The eight Standards for Mathematical Practices (SMP) outlined in the CCSSM underscore distinct habits that make mathematics more coherent and purposeful for students. The SMP also provide a learning experience that is more authentic to the work of mathematicians, rather than the typical 'plug and chug' approach where students memorize formulas and use them mindlessly in problems of the corresponding school week/section in the textbook. Specifically, these mathematical practices call for teachers to build students' capacity to:

SMP1. Make sense of problems and persevere in solving them

SMP2. Reason abstractly and quantitatively

SMP3. Create valuable arguments and critique the reasoning of others

SMP4. Model with mathematics

SMP5. Use appropriate tools strategically

SMP6. Attend to precision

SMP7. Look for and make use of structure

SMP8. Look for and express regularity in repeated reasoning

While grade-level *content* standards vary from state to state to best meet their students' needs, the practice standards are promoted in state standards nationwide because they attend to common learning struggles in mathematics. Though the CCSSM lists these practices separately, they are all connected, and teachers could likely address several of them in one same lesson.

A close look at the CCSSM description of each SMP reveals the role of communication in the classroom, not only between the teacher and students but also among students. This is necessary for mathematical reasoning in SMP3 and also critical for accomplishing many other skills, notably sensemaking in SMP1, quantitative reasoning in SMP2, and attending to precision in SMP6. For example, in SMP6, 'precision' refers to how reasoning is communicated, how clarifying questions are posed, appropriate use of mathematical terms and definitions, and precision in the judgment of claims. In SMP4, the new standards also aim to make mathematics relevant to students by helping them learn how to "apply the mathematics they know to solve problems arising in everyday life, society, and the workplace" (CCSSM, 2010, p. 7). This implies a significant change from the artificial problems in widely used mathematics curricula. Understanding how to create learning opportunities for SMP development has been a significant challenge, especially because this cannot be accomplished without facilitating fruitful conversations with and among students.

Embedded in the discussion of how these crucial calls can be realized is the complex issue of identity and culture. The mathematics educational community recognizes classrooms as spaces in which mathematical identities are formed as students see themselves in relation to the mathematics. These identities influence how they participate in class, make sense of the mathematics, and grapple and confront challenges. Supporting our students to continually revise their identity is key to mathematical instruction, because developing a particular stance toward mathematics is part of understanding the field (NRC, 2002). In this regard, mathematics educators and researchers agree that underachievement is neither located within the students nor due to their culture, but rather, to counter underachievement we must understand how schools can draw on the wealth of knowledge and experience students bring with them (Civil, 2002).

> **❝ Language education is well-positioned to support and be supported by learning in other subject areas. ❞**

Consider, for example, Hogan's (2008) study of the significant effects on the mathematical understanding of geometry of a middle-school girl from a native (Yup'ik) coastal village in Alaska, who learned from a curriculum that incorporated her Alaskan Native culture. Specifically, the unit on perimeter, area, ratio, and proportion focused on understanding the structure of fish racks and learning how to build them; fishing was integral to the girl's homelife and her local community participation. The mathematical concepts were taught using both Western and Yup'ik elders' ways of knowing and using math (e.g., with referent units from Yup'ik nonstandard body measurements). The teacher identified the student as high-achieving, motivated, and self-confident as a mathematics learner, judgments Hogan confirmed during classroom observations.

In stark contrast, when the girl learned with a new teacher following a traditional curriculum—which Jester (2002) reported lacked sociopolitical and historical understanding of cultural relevance—the teacher described her as hard-working, doing her best to follow the tricks to get right answers, but struggling with a D+ grade. Hogan confirmed the significant difference during her classroom observations. While acknowledging that the girl had previously developed a strong mathematical identity, Hogan underscored the following with the new approach:

There was no way for her to build on that knowledge, maintain that ownership, and enjoy that power once she was back in a Western-style classroom. (…) Different contexts highlight different parts of our identities and abilities. We grow into stimulating intellectual environments or retreat to familiar coping strategies in uninspiring surroundings (p. 111).

Thus, to help our students with new educational and societal demands, we must create learning opportunities that honor their interests, prior experiences, and cultural backgrounds—including the languages they speak and ways they communicate—and encourage them to use these for their learning at all grade levels and across all subjects.

Pause to Ponder

1. Considering the mathematical practices mentioned above (SMPs), do you think they could be fostered in your classes, too? If so, which ones and how?
2. Does the issue of identity and culture resonate with you in terms of how it affects language learning? If so, how do you address it in your classroom?
3. Looking back at sections (1) and (2), could we provide our students with coordinated learning experiences where they could deepen their understanding of both mathematics and languages and support the formation of their identity as learners? Think especially of how these practices could support students who come from different cultural backgrounds.

Similarly, science education has seen a demand for new standards that address the change in scientific practices, content, and core ideas students need to know for the new century. The Next Generation Science Standards (NGSS, 2013) were guided by new research on science, science learning, and the benchmarks for science literacy from the American Association for the Advancement of Science. They are also based heavily on the National Research Council's Framework for K-12 Science Education (NRC Framework, 2012), which emphasizes the long-term impact of a solid science foundation: "Science learning in school leads to citizens with the confidence, ability, and inclination to continue learning about issues, scientific and otherwise, that affect their lives and communities" (pp. 286-287). The integration of a set of science and engineering practice standards, introduced by NRC, makes the NGSS differ markedly from prior standards documents. As in mathematics, the practices are interrelated and must be used across all grade levels.

We must note the clear focus on communication here. For example, students must learn to ask scientific questions answerable with empirical evidence, including that gathered by others or through investigation, and to *construct explanations and design solutions* that show their understanding of the implications of scientific phenomena: "developing their own explanations of phenomena, whether based on observations they have made or models they have developed, engages them in an essential part of the process by which conceptual change can occur" (NRC Framework, 2012, p. 68-69).

Pause to Ponder

1. Reflecting on these statements from the standards mentioned above, what Intercultural Competence elements might help foster communication in mathematics and science education?
2. Identify the similarities between the call in mathematics and science education for applications of classroom learning to the emphasis in citizenship education on action in the community in the 'here and now.'
3. How might an international perspective from language teaching complement mathematics and science education?

Furthermore, a teacher must engage students in *argumentation* that involves comparing information, explanations, and evidence so they can evaluate claims. NGSS calls for students to engage in scientific argumentation for both understanding science and learning "how to apply science and engineering for the benefit of society" (NGSS, 2013, p. 13). That is, argumentation and communication are central to the betterment of mathematics and science education.

The rapidly changing world's new demands have also caused social studies curriculum standards revisions. According to the National Council for Social Studies (NCSS), "[t]he primary purpose of social studies is to help young people make informed and reasoned decisions for the public good as citizens of a culturally diverse, democratic society in an interdependent world" (2010, p. 3). These new standards incorporate current research into previously established and revised curricular themes and adapt them to 21st-century needs. For example, the NCSS call for students to:

- hold conversations with people from different cultural backgrounds to gain a deeper understanding of culture (theme 1);

- examine how the environment (e.g., weather) and human population (migration) influence one another to make informed decisions on issues arising from human-environmental relationships (theme 3);

- understand others and their beliefs, feelings and convictions when exploring personal development and identity (theme 4);

- determine how they can contribute to the shared goals and desires of society as part of their understanding of how institutions affect their lives (theme 5);

- study rights and responsibilities, as well as the needs of social groups, that help them address the persistent issues and social problems encountered in public life (theme 6);

- gather and analyze data to systematically study unequal distribution of resources in an interdependent world economy (theme 7);

- examine the effects of global connections at the local, national, and international levels by interpreting the patterns and relationships of increased global interdependence and its implications for different societies, cultures and institutions (theme 9); and

- become familiar with civic ideals and practices in other countries as an essential component of active participation in our democratic society (theme 10) (pp. 21-30).

Pause to Ponder

Consider the points cited from the Social Studies Standards document and identify the common terms and ideas with those we have listed in our explanation of competences for Intercultural Citizenship. How can language education complement Social Studies, for example, by emphasizing Intercultural *Communicative* Competence and an international perspective?

Conclusion

In this chapter we have introduced and explained the theories and models of Intercultural Competence and Citizenship, providing definitions of essential concepts to give a firm foundation for the following chapters. We hope to have presented this in a way useful to you in your practice and encouraged you to think about how this can help you to be more systematic and explicit in developing further what you perhaps already do. We have also described ways other school subjects are transforming to adapt to the needs of the changing world. These represent substantial changes for teaching and learning of these subjects, but the commonalities with the goals and objectives of language education and Intercultural Competence are clear. We believe that these changes lend themselves naturally to a collaborative effort you can make with colleagues across different subjects/disciplines. In the next chapter, we discuss how this can be done.

An interdisciplinary approach to Intercultural Citizenship
—KEY COMPONENTS

Today, where everything is interconnected, what you can do with others is more essential than ever (Ashdown, 2012, https://www.youtube.com/watch?time_continue=960&v=zuAj2F54bdo).

This chapter presents the overarching ideas to consider when practicing the theory presented in Chapter 2. It is also designed to facilitate your dialogue with teachers of other subjects about an interdisciplinary approach to teaching for Intercultural Citizenship. For this purpose, it breaks down the key components involved in planning an Intercultural Citizenship unit:

1. Preliminary considerations
2. Theme for the unit
3. Unit purpose and learning objectives
4. Assessment plans
5. Core activities
6. Discipline-specific contributions, learning objectives, and curriculum standards

To illustrate how these components appear in practice, this chapter uses a unit that results in Scenario A from Chapter 1. This unit presents key discussion points, describes specific tasks for the classroom, explains the theory, and recommends instructional resources that support the interdisciplinary effort. This chapter also introduces important considerations specific to the language classroom, which are explored in Chapter 4 in its focus on detailed lessons for the language classroom through presentation of a new interdisciplinary unit on Intercultural Citizenship.

We agree with the late Paddy Ashdown, a British politician and diplomat who worked in Bosnia after Yugoslavia's dissolution, that today, more than ever, we must come together and collaborate to solve problems. If we do our job right, we can help our students communicate with those who speak a different language, hold a different opinion or come from a different cultural background, but also help them become mediators for people who otherwise could not communicate with each other. In Chapter 1, we shared snapshots of outcomes of units planned on the theoretical framework of Intercultural Citizenship, where mediation is central, as explained in Chapter 2.

Pause to Ponder

If you go back to the four scenarios in Chapter 1, can you find evidence that the students showed they were mediators?

In this chapter we will walk with you through the key components of planning an interdisciplinary unit for Intercultural Citizenship. To help us highlight them tangibly, we will use the Global Water Crisis unit. We invite you to re-read Scenario A, for it exemplifies a sophisticated approach to collaborative design across four different school subjects, or disciplines, with a common organizing theme. Before we dive into the key components of this interdisciplinary unit, we would like to offer an overview of it. (Subsequent sections contain finer details such as core activities, assessments, curriculum standards, etc. Daily lesson plans will not be presented here, as this chapter emphasizes developing interdisciplinarity. However, if you are interested in the details, at the end of this chapter is a resource that illustrates how one group of teachers created daily lessons for another global water crisis unit. Additionally, the next chapter has some more detailed planning of a complete unit based on Scenario B that was presented in Chapter 1.)

Overview

The Global Water Crisis unit aims to develop students' Intercultural Competence and Citizenship by engaging them in critical analyses of significant water issues using the lenses of different subjects and challenging them to become agents of change. The unit builds students' capacity to collaborate with others to investigate the water crisis, with the goal to create a final product they present to a larger community outside of the classroom. In their investigation students incorporate strategies, tools and knowledge from various school subjects that help them address different influences on water issues. Students work across all subjects around this unifying theme toward the collective final product. The work in each subject supports understanding of content knowledge essential to the discipline while also facilitating development of fundamental skills for intercultural communication that are crucial to integrate and develop ideas across all disciplines.

The work in the language classroom is vital for this unit's success as students learn to communicate their understanding of this global problem (and the various local consequences) with students from different cultural backgrounds. They become curious about how others perceive the water crisis, how different cultural backgrounds affect these perceptions and potential solutions. They use this information to analyze their self-awareness to better understand the water crisis, as well as learn appropriate ways to share their knowledge with others and make critical comparisons and interpretations so they can learn more from and with each other.

Probing students to explain their thinking in the TL enables them to search for clarity in their own and others' thoughts, expand the scope of information and analysis, and develop their ability to synthesize. They also gain new perspectives, inquiries, and ideas from students of other regions or different opinions and perspectives within their immediate communities. If students use another language, they need to be clear in both their communication and what exactly they want to say. They must thus reflect on how well they understand the content.

In the language class, students bring together what they learn in other classes to support and question their ideas for the final product. Figure 3.1 below presents a broad view of the unit showcasing a summary of the contribution from the different subjects involved.

Figure 3.1: Summary contribution of all subjects to the Global Water Crisis Unit

Foreign Language
Look for and explain different perspectives and factors influencing the water crisis around the world; discuss its local and global impact; propose solutions that can be supported with the knowledge gained across disciplines; raise awareness and propose action items for the local community that are informed by the interdisciplinary knowledge.

Science
Explore watershed models, water pollution, freshwater shortage; understand water purification processes, water conservation alternatives, advantages, limitations, and consequences; search for feasible solutions to specific local and global water issues that are supported by this scientific knowledge.

Interdisciplinary Intercultural Citizenship: Global Water Crisis

Social Studies
Describe distribution of natural water resources around the world; explore human impact on the structure and functions of water systems that influence the water crisis; search for feasible solutions to sustain and restore water resources in the local and in a foreign region.

Mathematics
Collect, interpret, compare, and represent data relevant to local and global water issues (e.g., consumption conservation, distribution) using ratios, rates, and proportions. Propose feasible solutions to specific local and global water issues that are supported by the mathematical analyses of data.

Key Component 1: Preliminary Considerations

At the start of the planning process, you will think about topics and themes in your curriculum that would help develop the Intercultural Citizenship of your students. These will likely relate to issues and concerns that affect the lives of your students and the communities in which you and they live. Thus you could find out about their interests or even ask them directly which topics move them. Before you plan any further, we urge you to ask the following guidepost questions for designing an interdisciplinary Intercultural Citizenship curriculum:

1. How will you ensure that your students have opportunities to:

   ■ acquire new knowledge and understanding of 'products, perspectives and practices,' as described in the *World-Readiness Standards*, related to the topic/theme?

   ■ discover for themselves the practices of people in other regions and contexts?

   ■ compare and contrast perspectives in different contexts on the issue in question?

   ■ analyze and evaluate products and perspectives that influence practices, and vice versa?

   ■ take or plan informed action in their (local, national, or international) community?

   In addition, as you think of lessons that might address the questions above, we recommend that you also consider the following questions proposed by Clementi & Terrill (2017, p. 68)

2. How will the lesson be:

   ■ goal focused?

   ■ learner-centered?

   ■ brain-based?

3. How will the lesson provide opportunities for:

   ■ critical thinking and problem-solving?

   ■ creativity?

   ■ collaboration?

   ■ communication?

   ■ assessment/feedback?

4. How will this lesson be part of a unit that is:

   ■ communicatively purposeful?

   ■ culturally focused?

   ■ intrinsically interesting?

   ■ cognitively engaging?

   ■ standards-based?

Clementi & Terrill (2017) provide a convincing research-based introduction to why and how to create 'brain-based' lesson plans that expose students to cognitively challenging activities, introducing something new rather than covering predictable content. Other considerations include:

- when and how much input is given in a lesson;
- how long students can process information in their working memory,
- when and how to move into more independent learning practices.

Key Component 2: Theme for the Unit

An interdisciplinary unit's success pivots around its use of different disciplinary perspectives that advance understanding beyond a single discipline. Key to achieving this is the selection of the unit's theme, since most complex questions will automatically require our students to draw from skills and knowledge they acquire(d) in other disciplines/subjects and from experiences in their daily lives.

Language teachers in the US are familiar with the notion of 'essential questions' as a means of planning themes and topics, but this approach may not be known to teachers in all disciplines. McTighe & Wiggins (n.d.) describe seven characteristics of good 'essential questions':

1. *Open-ended;* that is, not having a single, final, and correct answer;
2. *Thought-provoking* and *intellectually engaging*, often sparking discussion and debate;
3. Calling for *higher-order thinking*, such as analysis, inference, evaluation, prediction, unanswerable by recall alone;
4. Pointing toward i*mportant, transferable ideas* within (and across) disciplines;
5. Raising *additional questions* and sparking further inquiry;
6. Requiring *support* and *justification*, not just an answer; and
7. *Recurring* over time, worthy to revisit repeatedly (McTighe & Wiggins, n.d., p. 11).

Pause TO Ponder

1. In the seven characteristics of good essential questions above, do you see connections to Intercultural Competence and Citizenship? Could the questions help support the development of the knowledge, skills, and attitudes required for Intercultural Citizenship in language teaching?
2. More generally, how could essential questions support an interdisciplinary approach to teaching?

Essential questions are useful, because they help us and students connect what they learn with the bigger picture all along their educational path, as essential questions can be revisited. When there are no simple answers we and our students are more likely to stay engaged. Moreover, more complex questions, as the seven characteristics indicate, foster critical thinking and the inclusion of knowledge from different disciplines. We can help students find reliable facts and justifications for their approaches to answering the questions, which supports their development of discovery and interaction skills, as well as interpreting and relating from the model of Intercultural Communicative Competence (Byram, 1997) introduced in Chapter 2. This in turn helps students develop their critical cultural awareness, which is central to Intercultural Competence.

Resources: Essential Questions

Clementi, D., & Terrill, L. (2017). *The Keys to Planning for Learning: Effective Curriculum, Unit, and Lesson Design* (2nd Ed.) Alexandria, VA: American Council on the Teaching of Foreign Languages.

McTighe, J., & Wiggins, G. (2013). *Essential Questions: Opening Doors to Student Understanding.* ASCD.

Sandrock, P. (2010). *The Keys to Assessing Language Performance: Teacher's Manual.* American Council on the Teaching of Foreign Languages. Alexandria, VA: American Council on the Teaching of Foreign Languages.

Wiggins, G. P., & McTighe, J. (2005). *Understanding by Design.* Alexandria, VA: ASCD.

Wilhelm, J. D. (2014). Learning to love the questions: how essential questions promote creativity and deep learning. *Knowledge Quest, 42*(5), 36.

In our example, the global water crisis is a central topic in science and social studies curricula that fits an intercultural unit across sciences, social studies, foreign languages, and mathematics. Moreover, we chose it because it is rich (see Additional Reading below), relevant to students' lives, and an invitation for them to learn content essential to each subject. All of these attributes are fertile ground for developing Intercultural Citizenship with an interdisciplinary approach that lets students learn about the topic from multiple perspectives and use this knowledge to take action on a problem of their choice—e.g., clean water accessibility or water conservation—that will result in a positive impact on their community and the world.

The theme need not be a specific topic from one of the subjects' curricula. Most topics are interdisciplinary; indeed, some of the topics most frequently addressed

Additional Reading

Global Water Crisis

The link below takes you to a National Geographic article that succinctly describes the current breadth of the global water crisis:

- https://news.nationalgeographic.com/2018/03/world-water-day-water-crisis-explained/

in the language classes (e.g., food, transportation, sports) can be easily addressed interdisciplinarily, being versatile enough to:

- use and advance understanding specific to each subject area/discipline involved;

- allow the application of knowledge acquired in one subject/discipline to another, each enhanced by the other;

- prompt students to reflect on and challenge their own and others' ideas using the interdisciplinary perspective and their own experiences;

- allow students of different cultural backgrounds to collaboratively grapple with and critically analyze contemporary societal issues in their historical development, as well as problems of local and global concern, using an interdisciplinary approach.

Key Component 3: Unit purpose and learning objectives

Once you have selected the unit's theme, determine the unit's purpose and associated learning objectives. Language educators will find it helpful to plan the respective Can-Do Statements as learning outcomes for their students.

As explained, the Global Water Crisis unit's core purpose is for students to develop Intercultural Competence by investigating a specific water issue affecting their community, using their skills and knowledge from other subjects (hence an interdisciplinary approach). The aim is to help them understand the problem's causes and effects at the local and global levels, compared with water issues in other places, as well as to engage the students in thoughtful discussions with their classmates, with students from a country where the TL is spoken, and/or with students in a third country who are learning the same language and using it as a *lingua franca*.

Armed with this knowledge and combined perspectives, students collaboratively seek to increase awareness of the water problem affecting their community and to propose concrete action to improve the conditions at the local and global levels. The results of these efforts are presented in a public forum, such as the radio show presented in Scenario A. This last part is driven by the theory of Intercultural Citizenship; students change or develop a new perspective on an issue and apply their Intercultural Competence to a problem in the here and now.

There are no national curriculum standards for interdisciplinary teaching and learning yet, but there are specific learning outcomes in this example based on the theories in Chapter 2 that this unit targets. Specifically, by the end of the unit, students will first be able to:

- acquire for themselves new knowledge and understanding of products, perspectives and practices related to the global water crisis in their own community and elsewhere.

- discover for themselves the practices of people in their own community and in other regions in the world.

- compare and contrast perspectives and practices that affect water conservation at the local and global levels.

These outcomes are taken from a world languages perspective; the reader will recognize the reference to 'products, perspectives and practices.' The following ones are derived from citizenship education, where the key words are 'community' and 'other regions' together with 'take action':

■ analyze and evaluate potential solutions to the water crisis in their community and in other world regions.

■ take local community action informed by international perspectives to propose solutions to the local water crisis and their effects at, local, national and international levels.

We recognize that acquiring and discovering are difficult outcomes to assess using quantitative approaches and measurements but we believe that these are significant educational purposes which must be nonetheless pursued.

Pause to Ponder

Now that you have a better sense of the rationale behind the second and third components, we invite you to think about the scenarios in Chapter 1 and then look into your specific context to reflect on how these would play out for you.

1. Can you identify the main theme for each scenario presented in Chapter 1? How does each address the characteristics of a versatile theme listed earlier under Key Component 2?

2. If you were to create an interdisciplinary intercultural unit, which theme(s) would you like to consider? Thinking back again to the characteristics referred to above, does your selected theme address them?

3. If you were to create an interdisciplinary intercultural unit, what would be the purpose and learning objectives for such a unit? Which other subjects would be important to involve?

Key Component 4: Assessment Plans

Once the learning objectives are identified, focus on how students can show achievement of these objectives at the unit's end. When it is interdisciplinary, create an authentic assessment that addresses not only the objectives for each subject area but also the interdisciplinary objectives that correspond to the unit's purpose. In other words, the students must be able to apply what they learned in authentic ways that reflect the complexity of "real problems." That will likely necessitate interdisciplinary views, thus help students understand the reasoning behind this approach.

In world languages, summative assessment must focus on what students 'can do' with their Intercultural Citizenship knowledge, skills and attitudes in the TL. Here we recommend integrated performance assessments enabling the students to demonstrate their performance level in the three modes of communication using real world activities (for suggestions, see the 'Using can-do statements in assessments' sidebar below and the literature in the Additional Readings box).

Using can-do statements in assessment

In Scenario A in Chapter 1, where students are interviewed about their work on water consumption and its environmental effects in their own and another country, they expand their understanding of the local situation with the perspectives they gained from exploring and discussing these issues at the global level in the TL with students from another country.

Using the *NCSSFL-ACTFL Can-Do Statements* introduced in Chapter 2, they now must explain perspectives in another country as described by an Advanced level indicator:

Performance indicator: I can demonstrate awareness of subtle differences among cultural behaviors and adjust my behavior accordingly in familiar and some unfamiliar situations.

Furthermore, because the students are outside the classroom and engaging with their community, they also explain, in English, how they gained understanding, through working in another language, of their partners' perspectives in a way that will be clear to listeners. Their success in this depends on their ability to bring those perspectives to bear in the suggested solutions and plans for actions they present.

In Scenario B in Chapter 1, in which students explain in Spanish and English the need to prepare for natural disasters to members of the local community, they demonstrate their ability to interact in a cognitively and emotionally engaging way at an Advanced level of Intercultural Communicative Competence, sometimes with the help of teacher scaffolding.

Advanced interact benchmark: I can interact at a competent level in familiar and some unfamiliar contexts.

Performance indicator: I can converse comfortably with others from the target culture in familiar and some unfamiliar situations and show some understanding of cultural differences.

Students are aware of how some people they talk to may have relatives and friends in the regions where Hurricane Maria raged. So these students must understand the effects of this in their conversations.

In Scenario C in Chapter 1, students act as mediators for their immigrant families, helping them to understand the demands of everyday life in the U.S. and how they can manage these with their budgets and qualifications. They can analyze their own accomplishments at the Advanced level:

Advanced investigate benchmark: In my own and other cultures I can explain some diversity among products and practices and how it relates to perspectives.

Performance indicator: In my own and other cultures I can explain how a variety of products of public and personal interest are related to perspectives.

Performance indicator: In my own and other cultures I can explain how a variety of practices within familiar and social situations are related to perspectives.

They explain to their immigrant families what is normal practice with respect to living conditions, for example, and what ideas and 'perspectives' lie behind the normal expectations of what kinds of apartments they can hope to rent. Other approaches to assessment and the use of can-do statements have been introduced in Europe and are described in Appendix 3.1.

Activities for formative assessments are interwoven in all classes to assess not only content knowledge but also students' development of Intercultural Citizenship to inform any necessary modifications that would move students forward in any areas where further development is needed. Some activities students engage in across all subject areas are described below.

Reflection journals. Students write journal entries as they pass key benchmarks in understanding the water crisis. Prompts are provided for them to reflect on these benchmarks from each subject area's perspective. These reflections may focus on individual work they do in class or as homework, or they may be geared toward assessing students' understanding after group work has taken place.

As a language teacher you may have to make decisions concerning the use of the TL. In this example, students in middle school might be at the novice level of proficiency. With scaffolding they could perform at Novice High or Intermediate Low in specific tasks for which they acquired specific vocabulary and practiced interactions. That means they could add short reflections in the TL. A practice that has helped us in other projects is to let students use their L1 or a mix of L1 and the TL for reflections outside of class. This is consistent with the NCSSFL-ACTFL Reflection Tool for Intercultural Communication, which recommends that teachers allow students to reflect outside of class in their L1 in a way that can later be followed up in-class in the TL.

As an example aligned with the Reflection Tool at the middle school level in the Global Water Crisis unit, students can be assigned to reflect on the questions below, once they have explored issues and solutions to the water crisis around the world and in their own communities.

1. Describe three to five important water problems in places other than our own.
2. Describe three to five important water problems around us.
3. How do those problems compare? What do you think accounts for some of the differences?
4. Name some ways in which water problems are being combated or prevented. Where are these actions taking place?
5. How practical would it be for us to incorporate one of those ways in our community?
6. What are some ideas you have come up with to address the water issue in our community?

7. What new insights about our own place and other places around the world have you gained from thinking about this?

Educators themselves must also reflect on questions such as these, to help them formulate unit objectives and goals, devise assessment plans, create lesson structure, select supplementary resources, and clarify their expectations about the depth and extent of the students' products.

Another option is to ask students to use pictures (e.g., on Instagram) to reflect on questions by inventing simple captions. This will especially help students of lower proficiency levels. Representing their findings numerically, e.g., in graphs, bar charts, statistical tables, would be another way to help students reflect on the complexity of the issue without having to use complex language.

Interdisciplinary portfolio. Naturally, each subject area should be infused with formative assessment activities that target specific content knowledge students should be learning in the course of the respective units. From the start of the unit students keep an interdisciplinary portfolio containing such products as essays, reports, problem sets, short quiz questions, and exit slips from all subjects that feature landmark work, notable findings, and/or evidence that will serve to support the unit's final product, regarding both the specific water issue focus and the proposed action component. This portfolio also illustrates the interconnectedness of the subjects regarding water crisis solutions.

Progress reports. These are part of the interdisciplinary portfolio. Students write these reports for each subject area involved, describing what they know, including evidence from different perspectives, citing sources. They also reflect on what they still need to learn and how they can do so, as well as the roles of the specific subjects and their contributions to the solution and action plans. Language teachers may provide a template that enables language learners to capture complex thoughts in simple language, because the form structures the information and aids understanding.

Presentation materials and delivery. As students focus on the final outcome of an activity or action in their community, they consider how they will present what they have learned to an audience that likely lacks previous knowledge of the subject. This involves decentering, i.e., thinking from the perspective of their audience and deciding how to structure their presentation or other activities accordingly. This will also require rehearsal and assessment of the ways they learn from rehearsal and modify their activities, rather than assessment of the activities themselves. This assessment can come from their peers, which takes us to the next section.

Peer feedback. Assessing how students provide feedback to their peers is crucial. This includes guidance about how to do this appropriately in different subjects and how to provide productive, thoughtful feedback that lets others move forward in their understanding and/or identify areas needing further details or explanation. Feedback may be sought from classmates and/or outside peers working with each group. Prompts for this type of feedback may include: "What I understand from this group's presentation is..." *[Ce que je comprends de cette présentation est...]* and "What I do not understand from this presentation is..." *[Ce que je ne comprends pas de cette présentation est...].* Language teachers provide tools for asking for clarification, another key aspect of SLA.

Response to peer feedback. Assessing how students respond to feedback from their peers is also essential. This will help guide instruction on how to do this appropriately in different subjects, how to react in the moment, what to do while receiving feedback (e.g., take notes if feedback is provided orally), and what to do afterwards: identify what needs to be addressed and how and what might not necessarily require a change. This activity also leads students to practice Intellectual Humility (see side box), as students need to be open to criticism and evaluate what they know. This in turn will help them gain new knowledge. It might also make them better collaborators, as it is likely easier to work with someone who is open to criticism and able to consult others.

Intellectual Humility (IH) is a topic studied by philosophers in the area of virtue epistemology. One perspective on IH uses the notion of owning one's limitations, which focuses on awareness and attentiveness to our intellectual limitations, weaknesses, and mistakes. IH helps us know what we know and what we don't know, be open-minded to dissenting views, and counter arrogance and servility, which is described as a "lack of pride in one's own intellectual achievements which leads one continually to seek approval from those one judges to be better than oneself" (Tanesini, 2018, p. 28) The theoretical developments of IH have many connections to Intercultural Competence and Citizenship we have explored in our work. For further details, see the suggested additional readings. For the reader interested in more literature about Intellectual Humility, we recommend:

Baehr, J. (2013). Educating for intellectual virtues: From theory to practice. *Journal of Philosophy of Education, 47*(2), 248-262.

Wagner, M., Cardetti, F. and Byram, M. (2018) The humble linguist: interdisciplinary perspectives on teaching and assessing Intercultural Citizenship. In: Eva Luef and Manuela Marin (eds) *The Talking Species: Perspectives on the Evolutionary, Neuronal and Cultural Foundations of Language.* Graz: Unipress. pp. 419-443.

Whitcomb, D., Battaly, H., Baehr, J., & Howard-Snyder, D. (2017). Intellectual humility: Owning our limitations. *Philosophy and Phenomenological Research, 94*(3), 509-539.

Public presentation. In the Global Water Crisis unit, the culminating activity is a presentation in a public forum of the results of their investigations and a call to action based on their results. Assessment of this activity needs to consider how the public reacted, but those who assess must also know that difficulties may not be caused by weakness in the presentation. For example, some audience members may 'refuse' to understand because they are ideologically opposed to change or to specific changes students propose. At the same time, audience members may express genuine lack of understanding—or genuine appreciation of new insights provided by students—and these reactions should be considered in assessment.

Additional Reading

Assessment
The following resources are useful to create authentic assessment plans:

- Sandrock, P. (2010). *The keys to assessing language performance: Teacher's manual.* Alexandria, VA: American Council on the Teaching of Foreign Languages.

- Clementi, D., & Terrill, L. (2017). *The keys to planning for learning: Effective curriculum, unit, and lesson design (second edition).* Alexandria, VA: American Council on the Teaching of Foreign Languages.

Key Component 5: Core Activities

Planning also requires identification of activities to serve as the building blocks of the interdisciplinary intercultural unit. These activities help pave the way for the final products students are expected to generate, as well as informing the creation of the daily lessons for each subject area. By knowing these activities, the team of teachers may receive an overall view of how Intercultural Competence will be addressed in each of the subjects and determine the different opportunities for Intercultural Citizenship on both the interdisciplinary level and that of each subject area.

The main components of Intercultural Citizenship (Chapter 2) should help guide activity selection and design. The goal is to support students' development of the attitudes, knowledge and skills that foster their critical cultural awareness and help them generate thoughtful plans of action, substantially supported by all subjects involved, to address a critical societal issue. In our example, the following six core activities drive the interdisciplinary unit and inform the development of daily lessons for each subject area geared toward understanding and finding solutions to the global water crisis. You will notice that the activities offer opportunities for students to (a) delve deep into questions about water that focus on increasingly finer aspects as the unit develops, (b) evolve their understanding with small-group and whole-class discussions, and (c) reveal their understanding through different products such as written reflections, charts, posters, and presentations.

1. Water Footprint. This activity is a starting point for students to reflect on these questions:

    a. What are all the ways you use water every day?
    b. How much water do each of you use every day?
    c. What is your water footprint?
    d. What is the water footprint of our class? Our school? Our community?

e. About how much water is consumed in the United States of America every day?

f. How much of the earth's water is available for use by humans and animals?

g. What could help with water conservation? What can you/we do about it?

These entry questions can be posed in all of the different subjects involved. It is important to assess students' prior knowledge of and experience with the issue, by asking them to explore them in class or as homework. In the language class these are discussed in the TL, using links such as those in Instructional Resources 1 below. In beginning language classes students can also investigate the questions in English outside of class. The NCSSFL-ACTFL Reflection Tool recommends that the teacher follow up on these reflections by then providing tables or visual representations, using a few words in the TL to discuss water usage. Teachers of the various subjects can focus on specific questions, especially if the activity has already taken place in another subject area. However, please note the significance of discussing these questions in every subject, as each offers a particular perspective specific to each discipline that is crucial for an interdisciplinary unit such as this one.

Instructional Resources 1

Water Footprint Calculators (currently available at):
http://wecalc.org/calc/
http://www.csgnetwork.com/waterusagecalc.html
http://www.watercalculator.org/ (links to water usage, saving water, educative links, other languages)
http://waterfootprint.org/en (global network, sustainability, fair share, as well as tools, research, and data)

Calculators of water use in other languages (currently available at):
http://www.energies-nouvelles.net/calcul-consommation-eau/
https://fandelagua.com/huella-hidrica/
https://huelladeciudades.com/AppHHCali/main.html
http://www.gelsenwasser.de/wasser/wasserverbrauchsrechner/

Data on water consumption, American footprint, conservation initiatives and more (currently available at):
https://www.nature.org/en-us/what-we-do/our-priorities/protect-water-and-land/

The activity begins with a general brainstorming discussion of water consumption, reminding the students that this includes not only the cups of water they drink throughout the day but also water used, for example, when showering, hand-washing, rinsing a cup in the sink, or cooking. Students are then asked to calculate their individual water footprints. They can do this as homework, keeping track of the different ways water is used in their homes, using an online calculator to find their household's water footprint. Next time in class, students discuss their findings in pairs, comparing across their individual footprints and consumption habits. Together they investigate water consumption in their community and the country to understand similarities and differences, as well as the limitations of this natural resource.

Finally, a whole class discussion is facilitated for students to share their findings, calculate the water footprint of the class as a whole, and discuss causes and consequences of high water usage. Perhaps the community faces water use limitations itself, or students might know places where that is the case. If students are not familiar with water use limitations, we recommend sharing resources with them so they become familiar with the problem (see suggestions in Instructional Resource 1). (It is beyond the scope of this chapter to include detailed instructions that help learners use the TL to explore the topic, but in Chapter 4 we go into more detail regarding planning activities using the languages students are learning.)

This activity is the starting point for students to become aware of the global water crisis, piquing their curiosity about the different habits feeding into it, as well as engaging them in the search for solutions. The questions provide fertile ground for comparing and contrasting water consumption at the personal and local levels and beyond, and prompting initial ideas about water conservation.

In terms of Intercultural (Communicative) Competence, students are beginning to use their skills of discovery about themselves and others, use the TL websites to see if and how the focus differs in diverse contexts, and learn the vocabulary items by using them. The discussions will lead to reflection on perfunctory water-use practices in students' own homes and communities. This also entails the first stages of the critique involved in critical cultural awareness and the decision to attempt to introduce changes. Investigating the concepts in other subjects will help students access complex information.

Working on the same content in another language will help them pinpoint what they do not yet understand while giving them different perspectives and new information they can compare with other findings. We noticed that our students learned to understand complex concepts better when using simple language to explain them. This might be because they cannot hide behind language but, on the contrary, must be extremely clear in their thinking and simple in their explanations.

2. Water issues around the world. This second activity is geared toward expanding students' knowledge of the global water crisis by exploring other water problems such as pollution, scarcity, diseases, and more. This work is done as a jigsaw puzzle: first working in groups on a particular piece of the puzzle, then each group presenting and discussing their findings with the whole class. The aim is for everyone to grasp the entire puzzle picture by the end of this activity.

Students work in groups of 4 to 5, choosing a different set of issues surrounding water such as: pollution, scarcity, diseases, and/or conflict to investigate where they occur (using maps); their causes (human and/or natural); the number of people affected (use census data) and in what ways; and what is being done and by whom to combat the issues (government, public, private sectors). Group findings are presented and discussed with the entire class, allowing students to ask for clarification and further evidence if necessary (see Instructional Resources 2).

Instructional Resources 2

Estimations of water consumption per capita (currently available at):
https://water.usgs.gov/edu/qa-home-percapita.html

Where is your water hiding (currently available at):
https://support.nature.org/site/SPageNavigator/action_center/action_center.html

Water for life (currently available at):
https://www.nature.org/en-us/what-we-do/our-insights/perspectives/water-for-life/

Statistics about worldwide water consumption (currently available at):
http://www.watercalculator.org/footprints/water-footprints-by-country/

How to use infographics in their presentations (videos, samples, and infographics as assessment tools) (currently available at):
https://www.schrockguide.net/infographics-as-an-assessment.html

Supporting collaborative work (currently available at):
https://www.edutopia.org/article/strategy-effective-student-collaboration

In the language classroom, teachers scaffold the activity by providing resources for students to understand important vocabulary and grammatical structures, as students should have the opportunity to interpret what they read. This calls for comprehension checks and a variety of scaffolded activities to ensure their understanding. Strategies such as using tables to summarize complex materials will also help students think deeply and express themselves in the TL.

Where a project has been established with students in another country—one where their foreign language is spoken, or one using the foreign language as a *lingua franca*—they can share what they have found and learn from each other, as students will be reading and interpreting information from places not necessarily familiar to them. Hence, this exchange would let them grasp the problem better, as their peers lay offer new insights, interpretations or views they have developed elsewhere within and beyond the school. It also lets students develop tolerance of ambiguity if confronted with results different from what they expected, which is key to developing Intercultural Competence.

Students can also consult statistics about worldwide water consumption (see Instructional Resources 2). In comparing personal and country-wide statistics, students can be encouraged to analyze reasons for differences and discover more about habits, precautions, and/or activism practiced in other cultures, while learning about water problems in other parts of the world. Comparing and analyzing similarities and differences between the realities and experiences of different places is central to Intercultural (Communicative) Competence and Intercultural Citizenship, and lets them critically look at how they interpret information and ways their cultural background and knowledge influence their inferences. Statistics are also a tool for analyzing more complex information using simple terms (e.g., numbers, focused vocabulary).

In scaffolded activities, students can thus analyze complex issues at low levels of language proficiency.

3. *Water issues in my community.* Once students have gained substantial knowledge about water issues in their own region and around the world, they can start analyzing specific issues in their local community. Here they carefully think about the options for raising awareness, solving, and/or reducing water-related problems.

For this activity, students are divided into groups of four to five. Each group focuses on one issue surrounding water—pollution, scarcity, diseases, conflict, etc.—to investigate its severity in their community (or state or region), its causes (natural and/or anthropogenic), the number of people affected (use town or state census data) and in what ways, what is being done and by whom to combat the issues (government, public, private sectors). From this, the group develops two plans: (1) for raising community awareness of their specific water issue, and (2) for proposing actions the community can take to solve or mitigate it. Resources students can explore to better understand water issues specific to the local community include videos, magazine articles, and local organization websites (see Instructional Resources 3 for examples).

Students will learn strategies for exploring each of the aspects from each subject's perspective, and will learn to use the tools and methods from that discipline to gain a better understanding of the problems (see subsection 6). Each group prepares a presentation (e.g., report, poster, slideshow) to share the results of their investigations with their classmates and what they are thinking about as possible actions in their community. Students read articles and watch videos that familiarize them with water issues in different regions in the US including their own. They do this before investigating their own community, to better equip them with tools to search for suitable information, facts and data that best inform their progress.

In past projects, teachers of other subject areas became curious about vocabulary related to the topic in the TL. This lets students be teachers and indeed celebrate the interdisciplinarity. Such projects can look quite different each time they are used, depending on the decisions educators and students make about which aspects they want to emphasize and what information will be useful.

Groups present their results to the entire class so others can gain enough understanding of the case to analyze the problems from different perspectives, understand the reasons for similarities and differences compared to their own cases, and relate potential solutions or offer new ones. This decentering which is fundamental to intercultural communication will help the groups strengthen their presentations in preparation for the experience below. Where a project with students in another country or in the same country has been established, the presentations to each other will require TL skills as well as the decentering, which can be expected whenever the audience has different presuppositions. Language teachers can help students devise questions beforehand that will guide them in preparing their presentations.

Students must learn how to be respectful presenters and audience members. As presenters, they must know how to present their materials, receive and respond to questions, and handle potential differing arguments and criticism. As audience members, they must know how to pose thoughtful questions, bring up potentially differing views, and provide constructive feedback (see Additional Resources 3 for strategies). When they do this in another language, they must know how to use resources such as dictionaries. If they are presenting in English for a partner group in another country for whom English is a foreign language—or where they are using, for example, French as a *lingua franca*—they must learn how to consider their partners' language level. In either case students must be acquainted with rules concerning interactions.

For example, there are important differences concerning the appropriate language and procedures in situations of disagreement in different cultural groups. For example, if students are working on water quality improvement using a water contaminant that may affect the underground watershed in lesser ways than others, they can be guided by the science teacher, and through the language classroom, to control their level of language and incorporate knowledge about pragmatics in the different cultures. Scaffolding this activity so students practice the presentation comfortably and confidently is crucial. Practicing for the presentation and giving the presentations provide wonderful opportunities for students to use the TL meaningfully and authentically.

Instructional Resources 3

The videos and links below should help students become familiar with examples of water issues in some towns in the US.
Video: Water shortage and town's solution for Lompico, CA.
Search: What Happens If Your Town Runs Out of Water? (2014)
https://www.youtube.com/

Water Action in Connecticut (select your state) (currently available at):
https://www.cleanwateraction.org/states/connecticut

Students should also navigate relevant official sites for their own town or state such as the following departments:
- Zoning and Planning
- Transportation
- Energy and Environmental Protection

The following resources present some useful advise and methods for teachers to help students learn how to pose thoughtful questions, bring up potentially differing views, and provide constructive feedback is essential for this and many other activities we present in this book.

Freely accessible book *Peer Feedback in the Classroom* written by Starr Sackstein (2017). It covers many aspects important to scaffolding peer-feedback, including what it looks like, how to create a feedback-supportive classroom environment, and how to incorporate technology for this process. (Currently available at:)
**http://www.ascd.org/ASCD/pdf/siteASCD/publications/books/PeerFeedbackIn
TheClassroom_Sackstein.pdf**

Protocols can serve as an invaluable scaffold to help students learn to give and receive feedback. The link below is to a simple protocol that you can use and that can be easily tailored to your grade-level, translated to another language, or modified in other ways with your own students:

http://www.readwritethink.org/files/resources/lesson_images/lesson261/peer.pdf

Peer Review as a strategy, developed by the International Literacy Association, contains a brief overview of background research, a 'how to' guide, and additional resources. It can be currently accessed freely at:

http://www.readwritethink.org/professional-development/strategy-guides/peer-review-30145.html

4. Water issues in a community beyond their own. We have already suggested focusing on projects with students in other countries where the language being learned—e.g., French—is spoken or where other students are also learning French and it can be used as a *lingua franca*. Here we focus on water issues in the region where the foreign peers live. The opportunity to interact with peers in another country enriches students' experience, especially when they are in the early stages of language-learning with low proficiency levels. One option here is to encourage each group to use the language of their schooling that for the others is the TL. They must be aware of the limits in the TL of their partners and find ways to use the language to make it accessible to their partners.

In this activity, students are divided into intercultural groups, where different groups in the classroom are paired with groups of students from a community different from their own (determined in the world language class) who have also completed the activity described in (3). Students share the results of their investigations to help the other group reach a good understanding of the situation on their peers' community, using their knowledge and tools from world languages, science, math, and social studies. Students should prepare for this group work by reading about the water issues in their peers' region(s) and by generating talking points or questions they could raise during the discussion to ensure they understand the problem from different perspectives. We offer some ideas in Instructional Resources 4, below.

Instructional Resources 4

The site below shows water distribution around the world and include pages dedicated to water use, water quality, and water properties that students can use to generate interesting discussion points.

http://water.usgs.gov/edu/earthwherewater.html

The following video showcases the water crisis in South Africa
How Cape Town's Residents Are Surviving the Water Crisis (2018)
https://www.youtube.com/watch?v=XxZAqswJfL4

Here students can focus on Intercultural Communicative Competence, particularly on juxtaposing comparison and contrast to understand new perspectives and interactions that raise questions about what is 'normal' behavior, from the mundane question of how many showers one takes weekly to the major questions of governments requiring people to move out of their homes to create a new water reservoir.

N.B.: This should not be the first time students interact in these intercultural groups with one another. They should have had opportunities for exchanges in intercultural groups that would have prepared them for working together in a substantial exploration such as this. A 'getting to know each other' phase is crucial to develop the trust needed to work together (see Byram, Golubeva, Han, & Wagner, 2017 for examples of different phases in Intercultural Citizenship projects). Also, educators and students must prepare for misunderstandings and other bumps in the road. Such challenges often enable them to learn and practice intercultural competence.

5. Investigating solutions and actions—Intercultural Citizenship in practice. Working in the same intercultural groups as in the previous activity, students collaborate to deeply analyze the two contexts. Now that they have shared what they know about their respective places, they come together to identify similarities and differences in the effects of the issues each region faces. Students also collaborate to understand the reasons behind these comparisons, accounting for cultural, geographical, scientific, and social commonalities, peculiarities, and distinctions.

In the language classroom, this collaboration is facilitated using charts (see the templates in Appendix 3.2), which help them identify these comparisons and provide a basis for their discussions. Before filling out the charts, students take them to the subject area classes and discuss their understandings (in their L1) specific to each area, guided by the specialized teacher, to ensure that they have solid arguments for their observations. At this point students can then fill out the charts in the TL so they can work together to analyze their results. In this process, the language teacher guides them on different ways to formulate speech acts: defend, add, refute, etc. The aim is to come to a consensus using the TL.

In a similar way, they examine existing and prior efforts toward improving the situation in each context and the results these improvements have manifested in their communities. Sample resources students can explore to support and bolster their arguments are listed in Instructional Resources 5. Building on this work, together they explore different ways to bring awareness to their communities and engage them in actions supported by knowledge and tools from world languages, science, mathematics, and social studies. The goal is for the group to put forward one of these ideas that is well supported and suitable for their contexts.

Students work collaboratively to develop a product (e.g., advertisements, fliers, presentations, posters, banners) they can bring to their communities to make them aware of the need to alleviate the local water crisis in each community, as well as propose concrete ideas/activities to improve the situation. Students also anticipate potential resistance to their proposals and incorporate arguments or acknowledgments of these in their work. The intercultural group gives the final product feedback and suggestions for improvement, in preparation for a culminating activity such as the one described in Scenario A in Chapter 1. (An alternative option for a school focusing on engineering or one with a makerspace would be to build something that can help solve an aspect of the water crisis, e.g., a device that saves water when showering or a computer program that helps develop awareness about water use.)

Instructional Resources 5

Suggested sites for students to explore at this point:
Nature conservancy—Global Campaign
http://ourworld.nature.org/

The site below presents a campaign for the public, corporations and conservation organizations about freshwater, reduce water footprints and restore flows and health to vital freshwater ecosystems.
Students can also share their own tips.
https://businessforwater.org/engage

Nature Conservancy—Resources for educators including videos, stories around the world
https:/ /www.natureworkseverywhere.org/

6. Public Forum Presentation. This is the project's culminating activity. In a public forum each group presents the results of its investigations and a call to action based on the results. There are a variety of ways students can record/report their results for their presentations. They can create digital slideshows, videos, websites, digital or traditional booklets, etc. These may include additional works such as pamphlets, art pieces and/or practical demonstrations to complement their reports.

Students should be given many opportunities to prepare for and practice public speaking as well. Instructional Resource 6 suggests activities and exercises for your students. Insights and tips from experienced teachers, some of which can be modified to present to your students, can help as well.

For example, in the language classroom teachers can use the MEEET approach (Main idea, Example/Explanation, Example/Explanation, Example/Explanation, Takeaway) that Jory Krudler describes in the Edutopia article listed in Instructional Resources 6. This can help students structure their thinking about the issue at hand. Students select a random topic of their choice on which to give a short speech to the class in the TL. They are given time to brainstorm and outline the speech that follows MEEET. Each component can be adjusted to the students' level of language proficiency. We concur with Jory that the teacher should go first, modelling the speech for the students and then following that up with a walk through the MEEET outline the teacher created and followed. The teacher can then have everyone prepare a MEEET for a specific topic. Here you would choose one from a topic you have previously treated in class, and for which you know students possess the linguistic/communicative tools and the appropriate comfort level in the TL. All students create their own MEEET presentations, and a few volunteers present their speeches. This is followed by a whole-class reflection on the presentations, identifying what makes a good presentation, what helps or hinders it, and how to overcome challenges. Students can then create their own MEEET presentations and deliver them to small groups or the entire class. In this activity students learn important skills related to both the language and presentation in ways sensitive to contextual (including cultural) differences.

The venue for this presentation could be a radio show (see Scenario A), a town hall meeting at the local library, or a school presentation open to the entire community. Local museums and children's science centers are likely to sponsor such an activity in their temporary exhibit halls or dedicated educational rooms, and state colleges and universities have relevant locations that would support such a public event. Naturally you would need to decide upon and arrange the presentation venue in advance. We recommend that you involve your students in this process (e.g., selecting, advertising, conducting a pre-event walkthrough) to give them responsibility for the event's success. Here you can tap into existing network connections you and/or your colleagues from other subjects (or other schools) may already have in order to choose the best venue for your project.

In terms of Intercultural Competence and Citizenship, this activity enables students to communicate their findings and ideas to an outside audience, put their arguments to the test, receive (or ask for) further insights or questions about their ideas, and see whether or not the community will be able to take the actions they propose. That is, it lets students authentically practice their skills as mediators while validating what they learned as something useful and impactful here and now.

Instructional Resources 6

Public speaking preparation (currently available at):
http://www.edutopia.org/article/low-stakes-public-speaking-exercise
http://www.scholastic.com/teachers/articles/teaching-content/grades-3-5-public-speaking-activities/
http://languageartsclassroom.com/2015/04/public-speaking-activities.html
https://www.scholastic.com/teachers/lesson-plans/teaching-content/group-product-pitch-presentation/

Teacher Insights and Tips (currently available at:)
http://www.teachingenglish.org.uk/article/student-presentations
https://www.edutopia.org/blog/8-tips-classroom-presentation-jason-cranford-teague (geared towards teachers but tips can be adjusted for students)
https://study.com/academy/lesson/the-importance-of-presentation-skills-in-the-classroom.html
https://www.schoology.com/blog/7-best-presentation-tools-students

Key Component 6: Discipline-specific contributions, learning goals, curriculum standards

Once a common understanding of the unit as a whole interdisciplinary endeavor is envisioned, we focus on each specific subject, clearly identifying the learning goals and curriculum standards specific to each subject area involved and how these contribute to the overall goals. We presented a general picture of the different contributions in the Global Water Crisis unit overview (Fig. 3.1). Below we offer a more detailed description. For each subject area we offer additional information such as grade or proficiency level, main curriculum topic, a summary of the classroom focus, the individual learning objectives and the specific curriculum standards.

We hope these details will help you see how the unit is planned to support the development of content knowledge within each subject, but also how it builds content across all disciplines. Again, language teachers need not possess the knowledge presented in the different subject areas below. Your collaborator colleagues, as well as your students, will contribute it. Moreover, through our conversations we learn to understand our colleagues' objectives while also enriching our own personal knowledge and understanding of the world.

> **" The unit is planned to support the development of content knowledge within each subject... also...builds content across all disciplines. "**

We begin with the world language classroom and move through the other subjects one at a time. We describe here a constellation of interdisciplinary work that does not cover all possible combinations but focuses on those less frequently discussed and illustrated. (For an alignment between the National Standards for Learning Languages and the Common Core Standards in English Language Arts, visit **actfl.org/sites/default/files/publications/standards/Aligning_CCSS_Language_Standards_v6.pdf**.

Foreign Language Classroom Overview

Language: French

Grade level: 6–8

Language Proficiency Level: Novice-mid to novice-high

Essential Question: *Comment pouvons-nous mieux comprendre nos problèmes (par ex. la crise mondiale de l'eau) en comparant notre situation à celles des autres?* [How can we better understand our own problems (for example, the global water crisis) by comparing our situation with those of others?]

Here the distinction between proficiency and performance is key. Bong (2019) describes the difference between proficiency, performance and achievement:

> Simply stated, Proficiency is the ability to use language in a real-world situation, Performance is the ability to use language in a limited and controlled situation such as a classroom or controlled situation-based exchange, and Achievement is the ability to repeat language elements that have been taught and mastered at some level. Each has a role in language learning, but only proficiency is what people use to communicate in the real world. (p. 1)

> **❝ Teachers can facilitate performance at a higher level by carefully scaffolding activities and providing the tools necessary to complete tasks. ❞**

Although students' proficiency might be at a lower level, teachers can facilitate performance at a higher level by carefully scaffolding activities and providing the tools necessary to complete tasks (e.g., vocabulary, grammatical structures, visual representations, presentations skills). Students will thus be able to discuss the prepared topic and negotiate meaning because they collected the necessary information, vocabulary, practice structures, etc., in advance. For more information on the ACTFL performance guidelines and how to plan Integrated Performance Assessments (IPA), see Swender & Duncan (1998); Adair-Hauck, Glisan, & Troyan (2013); and the ACTFL Keys Series.

In the overview (Fig. 3.1), you, as a language teacher, will have noted how language classroom activities are integrated into the unit's overall development. These scaffolded activities include:

- students reading information about water consumption in other countries, using websites in the foreign language (Interpretive Mode of Communication, Interpreting and Relating);

- students comparing and contrasting their own statistics—their personal ones and those of their family, for example—with statistics provided by partners in an international and/or intercultural project (Interpretive Mode of Communication, Interpreting and Relating);

- discussing with their partners—or simply with their classmates in the world language classroom—their findings, conclusions, concerns and actions to take (Interpersonal Mode of Communication, Discovery and Interaction);

- preparing materials for dissemination in a community, some of which can be in the TL if a group of users of the TL exists within the local community (Preparing for Presentational Mode of Communication, Critical Cultural Awareness, Action in the Community).

It is the final element—preparing and taking action in the community, as discussed in the language classroom and/or with project partners—that unites all students have learned in the other three subjects into a structured final product that is understood as tangible (e.g., presentations) or intangible (e.g., discussions with parents or neighbors about what the community might do).

In the course of this work, students will also be able to demonstrate what they 'can do' in intercultural communication as described in the NCSSFL-ACTFL benchmarks for Intercultural Communication, e.g., in the Investigate dimension at the Novice level: *In my own and other cultures I can identify products and practices to help me understand perspectives.* (For more links to the Can Do Statements, see Appendix 3.1.) In addition, students should have opportunities to address questions that show how they use their knowledge of culture, as suggested in the NCSSFL-ACTFL Reflection Tool, with guiding prompts such as:

- Choose a water issue in which the way the people use the water seems to generate the problem.

- Explain how the issue affects cultural aspects in that community.

- How does this compare to the experience in your community?

- How might this be similar or different to another community?

Where students can be put in touch with their peers in other countries (e.g., through the Internet), even beginning students can interact with their peers. Teachers can help these students prepare for the interaction with their peers in advance with closely scaffolded materials (e.g., posters, short presentations with structured formats that require only novice-mid language, etc.). Each group can use its own language— which means the other groups must comprehend the TL—and each group must think carefully about how to formulate what they want to say so it is accessible to novice learners. Depending on your context and the students' proficiency levels, students can also interact with other groups of people (e.g., refugees in Scenario D, community members in Scenario B).

Let us now look at how the Science classroom can contribute to the students' understanding of the global water crisis.

Science Classroom Overview

Grade Levels: 6–8

Middle School Main Topic: Earth, Space and Science

In the science classroom, students explore the water crisis within the study of the Earth's systems and human impact. The aim is to understand the cycling of water through the Earth's system and human dependence on water. The science unit's perspective on the global water crisis will allow students to design and evaluate methods that apply scientific principles for monitoring and minimizing the human impact on water usage and pollution.

Specifically, students create models of the water cycle and use watershed models to help them understand underground water and its movements. They explore different ways to combat water pollution (e.g., dilution and chemical) and freshwater shortage (e.g., desalination). They investigate water purification (e.g., reactants) and water conservation (e.g., coagulation), and evaluate the advantages, limitations, and short-term and long-term consequences of their actions.

As students progress through the science unit, they conceive scientific explanations for how increases in human population and per-capita consumption of freshwater affect the Earth's ecosystems. Additionally, throughout the unit, students construct oral and written arguments using empirical evidence and scientific reasoning to support or refute explanations or methods for resolving significant and complex issues in water supply and use. Explanations, arguments, and solutions are supported by their own investigations, which use multiple variables and provide evidence based on valid, reliable data from trusted sources, including their own experiments.

These experiences support students' development of Intercultural Competence within the science classroom. They learn to communicate scientific ideas in ways that align with the discipline, focusing on such key tenets of Intercultural Competence as considering and making sense of different perspectives, interpreting and relating different approaches or techniques, and providing evidence to support their solutions. They also apply what they know to make a difference in their community, which advances their development of Intercultural Citizenship. By the end of the unit, students will be able to:

- describe the water cycle and characterize its key parts;

- identify how the different parts of the water cycle are impacted by human activity;

- explain the different ways in which water quality and access can be affected;

- compare and contrast features of different methods to improve water quality that are based on groundwater and its movements;

- find scientifically sound solutions to combat or prevent water pollution and shortage;

- evaluate the merit and validity of ideas and methods to combat water pollution and shortage and to purify and conserve this natural resource.

The specific science standards this unit addresses are summarized in Table 3.1 below. We use here the Next Generation Science Standards as a common framework, as each state would adopt its own standards based on these national ones. The specifics in Table 3.1 will help you and your science colleagues identify corresponding standards specific to your state.

Table 3.1: Next Generation Science Standards addressed in Global Water Crisis

Next Generation Science Standards

Performance Expectations

MS-ESS2-4.	Develop a model to describe the cycling of water through Earth's systems driven by energy from the sun and the force of gravity.
MS-ESS3-3.	Apply scientific principles to design a method for monitoring and minimizing a human impact on the environment.
MS-ESS3-4	Construct an argument supported by evidence for how increases in human population and per-capita consumption of natural resources impact Earth's systems.

Science and Engineering Practices	Disciplinary Core Ideas	Crosscutting Concepts
■ Asking Questions and Defining Problems ■ Developing and Using Models ■ Analyzing and Interpreting Data ■ Constructing Explanations and Designing Solutions ■ Obtaining, Evaluating, and Communicating Information ■ Engaging in Argument from Evidence ■ Planning and Carrying Out Investigations	■ ESS3.A: Natural Resources ■ ESS3.C: Human Impacts on Earth Systems	■ Patterns ■ Cause and Effect ■ Systems and System Models ■ Energy and Matter ■ Stability and Change

We now take a look at Social Studies and what natural connections exist with the topic here.

Social Studies Classroom Overview

Grade Level: 6th grade

Main Theme: Geography Human-Environmental interaction

Essential Question: How do human communities find ways to live sustainably in an environment with limitations?

In the social studies classroom the unit addresses human-environmental interaction from a geographical perspective, focusing on ways to apply geographic knowledge to the study of historical and contemporary developments and issues to help us solve problems related to the global water crisis and plan for the future. More specifically, the essential question is addressed by learning about the effects that the shape, location, and relationship of important bodies of water around the world have for human society, and learning about the consequences of human actions of the past to help them predict the likely results of future projects and activities that affect the hydrosphere. This can then be linked to the specific geographical areas students will have come across in language lessons.

Specifically, students research the hydrologic cycle, including groundwater as a source of water. In this process they examine the underground water cycle's stages to explain where freshwater comes from. Next, students explore the concepts of stream systems, the components and stages of streams as they make their way from an inland source to the sea, including the transfer of rock and soil particles. Students learn about the character of streams near the origins, mid-stream and near the mouth, as well as erosion and deposition. This knowledge allows them to investigate where, along a stream or river, human activities make most sense. Many different activities are considered: recreational (e.g., kayaking, rafting), life essential (e.g., drinking, fishing), industrial (e.g., cargo shipping, barge traffic), etc. If students work with others from a different context in either their own or another country, they can interview those other people about their water-related activities. You can see that much of the vocabulary needed for this activity is basic and useful for students.

Students also explore water construction projects (bridge, dam, port, wastewater treatment plant, hydroelectric dam) and identify and explain the parts of stream systems where it makes sense to build these. Many communities rely on bodies of water for their living. Students investigate different regions in the world to explain how people have made use of their sources of water and how they might have impacted those sources with different human activities and projects. Students are then guided to further explore the consequences of human action by examining farming and irrigation projects in several world regions to evaluate their benefits and negative impacts. They explore solutions to ease the negative impacts in the future.

Investigations of examples worldwide help students establish the universal applicability of natural principles and the possible wider reach of consequences from local actions. Another important aspect brought up in this final investigation is to understand how different approaches to similar environmental challenges are affected by cultural differences in perception, decision-making, and use of resources. Here students will see the links with what they have learned from their partners at an individual and personal level.

These experiences support students' development of Intercultural Competence within the social studies classroom where they learn the types of information, evidence, and arguments to consider from a social studies point of view. They also learn how their social studies education can help make a difference in their community that advances their development of Intercultural Citizenship. By the end of the unit, students will be able to:

- use deductive reasoning to discover how hydrologic system features impact human settlements;

- examine the causes/effects of water stream systems in human activities;

- justify why specific human activities occur in various regions depending on their water sources;

- evaluate locations in terms of suitability for activities;

- explain the impact of culture on the evaluations and alterations of the environment.

The specific social studies standards addressed in this unit are summarized in Table 3.2 below. We have constructed these from the Social Studies National Standards (NCSS, 2010), the C3 National Framework Dimensions (NCSS-C3, 2013), and the Common Core Standards for literacy in Social Studies (CCSS-ELA, 2010) as a common framework, as each state adopts its own standards based on these national ones. The specifics in Table 3.2 will help you and your social studies colleagues to identify corresponding standards specific to your state.

Table 3.2: Social Studies Standards addressed in Global Water Crisis

Social Studies National Standards

Theme 3: People, Places, And Environments
Social studies programs should include experiences that provide for the study of people, places, and environments.

Geography: Human-Environment Interactions—NSS-G.K-12.5
Environment and Society: Understand how human actions modify the physical environment/ Understand how physical systems affect human systems/ Understand the changes that occur in the meaning, use, distribution, and importance of resources.

GEO 6–7.3	Explain how cultural patterns and economic decisions influence environments and the daily lives of people.
GEO 6–7.4.	Analyze the cultural and environmental characteristics that make places both similar to and different from one another.
GEO 6–7.5	Explain the connections between the physical and human characteristics of a region and the identity of individuals and cultures living there.

Dimensions of Inquiry*

Dimension 1: Developing questions and planning inquiry
Central to a rich social studies experience is the capacity to develop questions that can frame and advance inquiry. Those questions come in two forms: compelling questions and supporting questions (NCSS-C3, p. 23–25).

Dimension 2: Applying disciplinary concepts and tools
The focus is on the disciplinary concepts and skills students need to understand and apply as they study geography. These disciplinary ideas are the lenses students use in their inquiries. The consistent and coherent application of these lenses should lead to deep, enduring understanding (NCSS-C3, p. 29).

Dimension 3: Evaluating sources and using evidence
Students need to analyze information and come to conclusions in an inquiry. These skills focus on gathering and evaluating sources, and then developing claims and using evidence to support these claims (NCSS-C3, p. 53–55).

Dimension 4: Communicating conclusions and taking informed action
Students should construct and communicate claims for a variety of purposes and audiences. These audiences may range from the school classroom to the larger public community (NCSS-C3, p. 59–62).

CCSS for ELA: Literacy in Social Studies – Grades 6–8

CCSS.ELA-Literacy.W.6.7: Conduct short research projects to answer a question (including a self-generated question), drawing on several sources and generating additional related, focused questions that allow for multiple avenues of exploration.

CCSS.ELA-Literacy.RH.6-8.4: Determine the meaning of words and phrases as they are used in a text, including vocabulary specific to domains related to history/social studies.

CCSS.ELA-Literacy.RH.6-8.7: Integrate visual information (e.g., in charts, graphs, photographs, videos, or maps) with other information in print and digital texts.

* NCSS C3 national frameworks (NCSS-C3, 2013)

Finally, we provide more details of the contributions that can be made in the mathematics classroom to support students' quantitative reasoning about the global water crisis.

Mathematics Classroom Overview

Grade Level: 6th grade

Mathematics Main Topic: Ratios and Proportional Relationships & Statistics

In the mathematics classroom the unit builds on the understanding that water is a limited natural resource that is non-renewable or replaceable over a lifetime. The unit focuses on proportional reasoning—mathematical approaches appropriate for understanding the relative significance of local and/or global water issues, analyzing data from official records and students' own explorations, and making decisions about missing data, relationships or representations to achieve a thorough understanding of the problem. Enhanced by the use of statistical content knowledge, these approaches give students tools to accurately compare, interpret and/or evaluate problems and potential solutions to the global water crisis, thus link directly with the Intercultural Competence skills of discovery, interpretation through comparison/contrast, and critical cultural awareness.

Specifically, students are guided to understand ratios as comparison tools to learn how much of the Earth's surface is water, relative to other components. Equipped with this knowledge, students explore how much of this water is available for human consumption by using proportional reasoning to understand the relationship between fresh and salty water, between freshwater that is ice, or shallow groundwater, or deep groundwater, and between freshwater in lakes and rivers versus water vapor in the atmosphere. Then they learn about historical changes in these relationships.

Students use different representations to predict potential future values of the different quantities if certain trends continue (e.g., ratio tables, double number lines). Their explanations and conclusions should reflect the limited availability of this natural resource compared to the immensity of the human population. As students progress through the unit, they analyze data on water use at home, in school (own investigations), and on a bigger scale locally and around the world (e.g., from official documents and reports and from their foreign language project partners). They look into how ratios and percentages can help understand the relationship between water use and water availability and determine which is better to help explain the effects of water usage and water shortage around the world. Students explore different paths to solve water issues and investigate which are most promising by scrutinizing them with proportional reasoning and statistical analysis approaches (e.g., variability and distribution).

In other projects language teachers collaborated with mathematics teachers, analyzed data collected for the world language classroom in mathematics, and discussed the visual representations created in the mathematics classroom in world languages in the TL (see, for example, Bohling, Wagner, Cardetti, & Byram, 2016; Byram, Conlon Perugini, & Wagner, 2013). It was especially meaningful that students collected and analyzed their own data rather than using examples with no connections to their lives.

Throughout this investigation students learn to use mathematical representations such as graphs, charts, and equations to understand which most effectively identify patterns in data or explain why certain approaches are better than others to highlight a specific characteristic that would support their suggested solutions to the water problems. Students are guided to generate solid explanations and viable arguments based on robust mathematical evidence and to provide critical feedback on explanations and arguments created by others.

These experiences are naturally related to students' development of Intercultural Competence. They support students' learning to communicate mathematical ideas in ways that align with the discipline and focus on important tenets of Intercultural Competence, such as considering and making sense of different perspectives, interpreting and relating different approaches or techniques, and providing evidence to support their solutions. In addition, students learn to use mathematics to argue for ways to make a difference in their community, which advances their development of Intercultural Citizenship. By the end of the unit, students will be able to:

■ use ratios to compare the extent to which different quantities affect the distribution of water.

■ identify when quantities should be compared using proportional reasoning to explain a certain phenomenon.

■ explain the significance of freshwater usage and availability locally and around the world using proportional relationships.

■ analyze data using statistical tools that help inform the extent of water issues in their own communities and in other regions in the world.

■ create viable mathematical arguments for possible solutions to different water issues at the local and global levels.

The specific mathematical standards addressed in this unit are summarized in Table 3.3 below. We use here the Common Core State Standards as a framework, as each state adopts its own standards based on these national ones. The specifics in Table 3.3 will help you and your mathematics colleagues identify corresponding standards specific to your state.

Table 3.3: Common Core State Standards addressed in Global Water Crisis

Common Core State Standards for Mathematics	
Ratios and Proportional Relationships	6.RP
Understand ratio concepts and use ratio reasoning to solve problems.	
6.RP.A.1.	Understand the concept of a ratio and use ratio language to describe a ratio relationship between two quantities.

▶▶▶

Understand ratio concepts and use ratio reasoning to solve problems. — *continued*

6.RP.A.2.   Understand the concept of a unit rate associated with a ratio a:b with b \diff 0 (b not equal to zero), and use rate language in the context of a ratio relationship.

6.RP.A.3.   Use ratio and rate reasoning to solve real-world and mathematical problems, e.g., by reasoning about tables of equivalent ratios, tape diagrams, double number line diagrams, or equations.

   a. Make tables of equivalent ratios relating quantities with whole-number measurements, find missing values in the tables, and plot the pairs of values on the coordinate plane. Use tables to compare ratios.

   b. Solve unit rate problems including those involving unit pricing and constant speed.

   c. Find a percent of a quantity as a rate per 100; solve problems involving finding the whole given a part and the percent.

   d. Use ratio reasoning to convert measurement units; manipulate and transform units appropriately when multiplying or dividing quantities.

Statistics and Probability	6.RP

A. Develop understanding of statistical variability.
B. Summarize and describe distributions.

6.SP.A.2.   Understand that a set of data collected to answer a statistical question has a distribution which can be described by its center, spread, and overall shape.

6.SP.A.3.   Recognize that a measure of center for a numerical data set summarizes all of its values with a single number, while a measure of variation describes how its values vary with a single number.

6.SP.B.4.   Display numerical data in plots on a number line: dot plots, histograms, box plots, etc.

Standards for Mathematical Practices

1. Make sense of problems and persevere in solving them.
2. Reason abstractly and quantitatively.
3. Construct viable arguments and critique the reasoning of others.
4. Model with mathematics.
5. Use appropriate tools strategically.
6. Attend to precision.
7. Look for and make use of structure.
8. Look for and express regularity in repeated reasoning.

Now that you have seen one approach to interdisciplinary intercultural teaching, we invite you to think about possible modifications and/or extensions that might better fit your context.

1. Adjusting for a different language, proficiency level, accessibility to foreign students (pen pal, exchange, or other programs)

2. Considering contributions from other disciplines such as arts.

3. Expanding to include other initiatives at your school. For example, makerspaces, Model UN, and others.

In Appendix 3.3 we have included a framework to facilitate your work with colleagues from other subjects when planning for an interdisciplinary unit containing the components mentioned above for preparing a theme and the teaching plans. Below are more examples of published interdisciplinary units you might want to use as starting points for your planning.

Additional Examples

Water—An Interdisciplinary Unit

This unit was developed by graduate students Nicole Coleman and Silke Gräfnitz from the Department of Literatures, Cultures, and Languages, and Steven LeMay from the Department of Mathematics, under the supervision of the authors and guidance from curriculum developers at West Woods Upper Elementary School from the Farmington Public School District in Connecticut. At the website below, you will find daily lessons for an interdisciplinary unit based on the social studies classroom with interwoven lessons in mathematics, Spanish, and science. This Global Water Crisis unit is accessible at **http:// globalwaterjustice.weebly.com/**.

Green Kidz—an international project

In a project involving young learners of English in Argentina and Denmark aged 10 to 12, the students focused on environmental issues. They investigated what they called 'green crimes' in their school and community, e.g., when people left computers running when not in use or threw away paper that could be reused or recycled. Each 'national' group then prepared a presentation for the other. After the presentation, they worked in mixed, 'international' Danish-Argentinean groups on a common project to create approaches to raising awareness of their concerns in their own communities. Finally, each 'national' group carried out various activities in their own communities using the ideas they had developed as an international group. The teachers and researchers involved wrote a full description of the project: "Green Kidz: Young learners engage in intercultural environmental citizenship in English language classroom in Argentina and Denmark" by Porto, Daryai-Hansen, Arcuri and Schifler. In: Byram, Golubeva, Han, and Wagner, (Eds.) 2016, *Education for Intercultural Citizenship – Principles in Practice*. Tonawanda, NY: Multilingual Matters

Conclusion

The important points to take away from this chapter:

- interdisciplinary approaches are based on an openness to collaborate, receive mutual help, and acknowledge with intellectual humility what we can learn from colleagues and students.

- all teachers can work within their own disciplines while contributing to the overall learning and activities of the students, who thus begin to see links and connections among subjects and the ways the combinations can be used directly in contributing to the life of their community.

- the language classroom gives particular force to decentering and discovering how issues are addressed in other languages and cultures, leading to comparison and questioning of what students otherwise assume is 'normal.'

- the language classroom serves as a means of bringing the work in other classrooms into a coherent whole with immediate implications and applications for their community in ways which are informed and enriched by the 'other.'

- the language teacher can lead these developments by helping colleagues see how their curriculum plans and demands can be integrated into a whole that makes sense to students.

We now have presented the theories that can guide your planning, as well as tools for interdisciplinary implementation, and an illustration of what this might look like in practice with the Global Water Crisis unit. We hope you can now see how the theories and concepts presented in Chapter 2 can lead to interdisciplinary work that is enriching for students and teachers alike. In the next chapter we take a closer look at another interdisciplinary intercultural unit that follows the key components outlined here. But this time we zoom in on the specific details of the language unit so you can see the week-by-week developments, connections to other subjects, and curricular standards it addresses.

Interdisciplinary connections in practice
—PLANNING FOR LANGUAGE TEACHING AND BEYOND

Many topics are not addressed in schools because of the breadth and depth of information accessible in a globalized, technological society. Much of the curriculum in textbooks is neither timely nor relevant to students' lives. Also, the daily schedule often fragments learning so that each teacher is given a defined time block to cover material that will likely be assessed on a state-mandated test. All of these hindrances make it difficult for teachers to engage students in studying any material in depth and to make connections between subject areas and topics (Coffey, 2009, p2).

This chapter presents the details for the language classroom of an interdisciplinary unit that incorporates Intercultural Citizenship, as described in Chapter 2 and planned under the principles described in Chapter 3.

Maintaining use of the TL as the medium of instruction, the unit builds up learners' Intercultural Communicative Competence and develops their Intercultural Citizenship so they can use it in the TL to impact the local and global community. This is done using a unit on natural disasters—specifically Hurricane Maria, which affected Puerto Rico in 2017—that leads to the outcome described in Scenario B of Chapter 1.

Chronological learning activities and assessments are described on a week-by-week basis. The weekly plans are supported with scaffolding and recycling of prior knowledge and skills and with readily available and prepared materials online. A sample unit plan is presented that includes the interdisciplinary connections to several other subjects. Templates showcasing handouts and blank forms have been added to the appendix to supplement this chapter.

This book focuses on giving students the opportunity to develop Intercultural Citizenship both inside the language classroom and outside across different subject areas, and to use their skills in the 'here and now' so they can understand and participate in the world around them. In so doing, we respond to the challenges we face as educators today, the challenge of relevance and the challenge of a holistic approach to learning as articulated above by Coffey. However, we are aware that such challenges are very demanding, and because we know that curriculum design is a time-consuming activity, we want to emphasize that units need not be created "from scratch." Rather, they can be built on prior versions of units, as is the example we present in this chapter.

❝ This action component helps students to immediately link what they learn in school to their lives beyond the classroom walls. ❞

In Scenario B in Chapter 1, students presented the fruits of their work in class, where they had studied the effects of Hurricane Maria in Puerto Rico and elsewhere to their local community. They wanted people in their community, whether Spanish-speaking or English-speaking, to see what they had done at school and how this could be of practical use for everyone. In this chapter we shall explain in detail how the students reached this point in their work and engagement with the life of their community, including the lessons and activities that led up to this public event.

The work builds on students' prior knowledge on a variety of topics—family, weather, housing, work, etc.—and incorporates the topic of natural disasters to include not only Intercultural Competence but also Intercultural Citizenship, i.e., an element of the teaching that would encourage learners to take some kind of action in society. As we explained in Chapter 2, this action component helps students to immediately link what they learn in school to their lives beyond the classroom walls, and the approach through citizenship education theory shows how language education can position itself to collaborate with other disciplines in schools and contribute to society in the here and now.

This unit was developed to be primarily conducted in the TL for high school students of Spanish at the Intermediate level of proficiency. However, it can be adapted to different levels and languages; with scaffolding and preparation the performance of students can be at a higher level than their proficiency level. That is, if students are assessed at a proficiency level of 'intermediate low,' they can still perform at a higher level in a prepared task for which they have acquired vocabulary and practiced interactions. Now it is time to unpack the curriculum to see how to build on learners' prior knowledge, practice, and experiences when creating a new unit of instruction.

Unit Details

The unit (or parts of it) can come after a variety of themes (e.g., weather, housing, family), thus building on what students already know about such themes in the TL. It can also apply what they have learned in other subjects about natural disasters, physical geography, states and countries, civilizations and customs, housing, building materials, and/or the environment. In particular, creating a link with mathematical skills and knowledge, the unit encourages students to reason quantitatively with data and their relationships to analyze and interpret information that will inform their arguments and conclusions.

However, for those teachers who are still exploring the notion of interdisciplinarity and do not wish to engage immediately in cross-curricular approaches, the unit can also be taught as a stand-alone, as it covers all aspects and objectives of Intercultural Citizenship. An essential guiding question that underpins this unit is, "What are the relationships between interdisciplinary knowledge of natural disasters and the quality of life in our interconnected contemporary world?" The unit deals with a specific natural disaster that occurred in September 2017 in Puerto Rico and the Dominican Republic and is shaped by the following questions:

- What were the effects of Hurricane Maria on Puerto Rico and the USA at the time the natural disaster occurred?

- What are the effects of Hurricane Maria on Puerto Rico and the USA to this day?

We start by identifying the desired results. We share some options here and invite you to come up with your own ideas based on your specific contexts:

- One option for an Integrated Performance Assessment (IPA) (Adair-Hauck, Glisan, & Troyan, 2013) is that, after interpreting a variety of authentic materials on Hurricane Maria, students plan and implement a presentation in a public or closed town-hall-like meeting in which they present their findings concerning the impact of Hurricane Maria on Puerto Rico and on their region, and in which they then discuss possible action items to address some of the remaining challenges, as described in Chapter 1. Students would invite Spanish speakers, and would be able to mediate in real-time and in the TL. [This could also be done as a role-play with students from other classes acting as the general public.]

> **❝ Students could plan a radio show in which they inform the public on the results of their investigation and invite the public to ask questions, or publish the results. ❞**

- Students could plan a radio show in which they inform the public on the results of their investigation and invite the public to ask questions, or publish the results.

As part of the unit, students could also be asked for their own ideas concerning potential actions and then decide together which ones they want to pursue.

Table 4.1: Summative Assessment

These tasks allow learners to demonstrate how well they have met the goals of the unit.

- The tasks follow the format of the IPA, but are integrated throughout the unit.
- The template encourages multiple interpretive tasks.
- The interpretive tasks inform the content of the presentational and interpersonal tasks.
- The tasks incorporate 21st-century skills.

Interpretive Mode		
Read, in groups, different news articles on Hurricane Maria, and prepare a summary for other groups who have not read the same materials, showcasing their understanding of a specific aspect of the hurricane that was introduced in the readings.	Watch, in groups, different videos on Hurricane Maria and prepare a summary for other groups, exposing their understanding and interpretation of what was suggested in the videos.	Analyze, in groups, different sets of statistics on Hurricane Maria, and prepare a visual presentation and interpretation for other groups, who have not analyzed the same statistics, illustrating their understanding of the data.

Presentational Mode	Interpersonal Mode
Work in groups to design a multimedia presentation on the effects of Hurricane Maria on PR and the region, using the summaries from readings and videos, as well as representations of the data provided from different groups' interpretations above.	(Teacher)-moderated meeting (of different classes or within the same class) in which students discuss possible action projects based on their findings on the effects of Hurricane Maria.

At the Town Hall meeting, students interact with their audience in a Q and A session after their presentation. |

As mentioned in Chapter 3, educators might ask the following questions to plan for teaching Intercultural Citizenship in an interdisciplinary fashion:

Will the students have opportunities to :

- acquire new knowledge and understanding of products, perspectives and practices related to the current content/theme?

- discover for themselves the practices of people in other contexts?
- compare and contrast perspectives in different contexts on the issue in question?
- analyze and evaluate products and perspectives that influence practices and vice versa?
- take or plan informed action in their (local, national, or international) community?

Also, any time you plan an interdisciplinary unit, reflect on the questions we presented in Chapter 3 posed by Clementi & Terrill (2017, p. 68):

1. How will the lesson be:
   - goal focused?
   - learner-centered?
   - brain-based?

2. How will the lesson provide opportunities for:
   - critical thinking and problem-solving?
   - creativity?
   - collaboration?
   - communication?
   - assessment/feedback?

3. How will this lesson be part of a unit that is:
   - communicatively purposeful?
   - culturally focused?
   - intrinsically interesting?
   - cognitively engaging?
   - standards-based?

We now provide an overview of the timelines suggested for the activities per week, followed by a chronological narrative of one of the ways this unit could be used. You may assign certain activities as homework, or offer shortened or more extended versions of them to accommodate to different contexts and settings. In the latter case, we encourage you to look into the planning questions posed above and to the theory presented in Chapter 2 to ensure that the important aspects of Intercultural Citizenship are successfully addressed. You are also encouraged to read Chapter 6, where we address frequently asked questions (FAQ) and offer practical tips about teaching languages for Intercultural Citizenship using an interdisciplinary approach, including suggestions for reaching out and working successfully with colleagues from other disciplines.

Overview of Timeline

Week 1
- Assessment of related vocabulary and background knowledge related to unit (family, housing, weather, work, migration, etc.)
- Pre-assessment of perspectives on natural disasters
- Introduction of natural disasters (group work, and each group just checks in a little more detail)

Week 2
- Introduction of eventual project;
- Hurricane Maria: Groups investigate different questions related to Hurricane Maria
- Start planning what information will be important to present
- Interview witnesses or friends and relatives of witnesses in the region

Week 3
- Continue investigation
- Based on their investigations and interviews, groups formulate a possible action plan relevant to their community/region
- Prepare presentation of findings

Week 4
- Present findings to other groups
- Students write reports to summarize what they have learned
- Groups work on synthesis of information

Week 5
- Invite participants, review logistics, obtain permissions (principal?), develop promotion plan
- Prepare handouts, pamphlets, posters, webpage and other promotional materials

Week 6
- Prepare presentation: What are the effects still today of Hurricane Maria? (different groups present different parts)

Suggestions for Materials

Week 1

We assess and expand on our students' knowledge of vocabulary related to the unit (e.g., family, housing, weather, work, migration). We also pre-assess students' knowledge of and perspectives on natural disasters, for example, by using questions that align with those suggested in the NCSSFL-ACTFL Intercultural Reflection Tool for high school students in the intermediate proficiency level:

1. Has your family experienced any emergency situations related to severe weather? If so, provide details to help explain what happened (Who? What? When? etc.).
2. Describe the types of extreme weather that are common in the region you live.

3. What are some of the measures your family uses to prepare for these types of situations?
4. Does your town prepare in the same way? Why or why not? What underlying considerations might come to play at the larger level?
5. Do you know of emergency situations related to severe weather in other regions, locally or globally? Explain.
6. Choose one of those and describe its impact on the region's migration movement, work force, health, etc. Were there consequences in other places? Which ones? For your own region? Explain.
7. What would you like to know about extreme weather in your region and around the world?

Using news articles, videos and other authentic materials available online, students are then introduced to the topic of natural disasters. Teachers may use slideshows or a vocabulary set available online (see Instructional Resources 1 below for sample materials to reactivate and introduce vocabulary related to natural disasters) or use their own method to review and introduce vocabulary, adding, for example, a sentence about the video on the aftermath of the hurricane.

In groups, students explore one disaster in some detail, drawing on skills of investigation/discovery that are concurrently emphasized in other subjects. For each group, the goal for the last lesson of Week 1 is to give a short presentation of their explorations (see Instructional Resources 1 below for ways to support effective group work). Each group creates a handout that includes a general description of their chosen disaster and its characteristics, a map showing where the most notorious disasters of this type have occurred, graphical representations that highlight important statistical information, etc. They have flexibility in choosing how to incorporate other important aspects of their chosen disaster. (Suggestions for this activity can be found in Appendix 4.1: Activity and guiding questions for group work)

> **"Students compare and contrast information considering all contributions, evidence, and logical reasoning as support for their observations and conclusions."**

After the presentation, the group facilitates a whole-class discussion to build common understanding and baseline knowledge of natural disasters, extending each group's work. The handouts provide a uniform structure to aid the comparison across all disasters. Students compare and contrast information considering all contributions, evidence, and logical reasoning as support for their observations and conclusions. They may also wish to compare with their own experience—direct or indirect, through social media for example—of a disaster and how people react to it.

All of these activities promote the development of Intercultural Competence skills such as comparison, discovery/investigation, as well as interdisciplinary skills from mathematics, science, and social studies, especially developing students' perspectives of the world.

Instructional Resources 1

Natural Resources

Resources to reactivate and introduce vocabulary related to natural disasters: a Quizlet set of vocabulary for natural disasters (currently available at): (**https://quizlet.com/18508325/spanish-natural-disasters-vocab-flash-cards/**) or an online slideshow with vocabulary (**https://study.com/academy/lesson/spanish-terms-for-natural-disasters-emergencies.html**)

Resources for pre-assessment: Video images of the aftermath of Hurricane Maria (currently available at): **https://www.youtube.com/watch?v=Y-Vqiu4liyE**

Resources with general information about natural disasters in Spanish to guide the group work (currently available at): **http://www.geoenciclopedia.com/desastres-naturales/**

Group Work

See Appendix 4.1: Activity and guiding questions for group work
Resources to support effective group work (currently available at): **https://www.edutopia.org/article/setting-effective-group-work**

Week 2

We introduce students to Hurricane Maria. We also introduce the summative assessment (see options of assessment in Instructional Resources 1 above) so students know what the end goal is. In addition, we share with them the rubric used to assess the final product and actively involve them in the assessment process. Together we discuss what we, as a class, think are important indicators of a quality product that show we have achieved the learning goals for this unit. We use this discussion to modify or add to the rubric, thus co-creating it with the students as a source of motivation and self-accountability for them (Sandrock, 2010).

Teachers may decide to use a video available online (see Instructional Resources 2: Video in Spanish, illustrating and modeling how to use data in meaningful ways) or prepare their own introduction for students to model how to use and analyze data in Spanish. Here students learn pertinent vocabulary and also see that they can express complex thoughts and concepts by using their knowledge of numbers and statistics and their background knowledge from other subjects. Thus they can stay in the TL without having to use complex vocabulary or grammatical structures.

We then provide authentic materials that introduce groups to different issues related to Hurricane Maria (see Instructional Resources 2 for some examples) and scaffold group work for students to develop ideas and start preparations for the final product that focuses on a specific aspect of the impact of Hurricane Maria in Puerto Rico or in the students' community. For example, students may decide to interview witnesses in Puerto Rico (e.g., using Skype) or friends, family, or contacts with a relationship with Puerto Rico and knowledge and/or experience with Hurricane Maria. In all of this they are guided to ask what reactions people had; for example, is it 'fate' and inevitable to suffer disasters? Can disasters be anticipated by scientific measures—and therefore the inevitable avoided? In this way students begin to see different beliefs and values beneath the reactions to Hurricane Maria. (Suggestions for extending this activity are offered in Appendix 4.2: Suggested extension to natural disasters around the world.)

The skills of Intercultural Competence are reinforced and expanded to include discovery in real time, comparison, and critical cultural awareness. These activities rely on and use interdisciplinary skills from mathematics, especially to reason quantitatively, use proportional and algebraic thinking, and interpret and represent graphs and statistical analysis. Students also use skills from social studies and geography to understand where people, places, and resources are located and why they are there, and to explore the relationship between human beings and their environment.

Instructional Resources 2

Hurricane Maria

These are suggested resources for different perspectives specific to Hurricane Maria (currently available at):

Video in Spanish illustrating/modelling how to use the data in meaningful ways: **https://www.youtube.com/watch?v=hhUvtP-hOgQ**

News article showcasing Hurricane Maria in numbers and pictures: **https://www.univision.com/puerto-rico/wlii/noticias/huracan-maria/en-numeros-oficiales-y-fotos-asi-va-la-recuperacion-de-puerto-rico-a-un-mes-de-maria-segun-el-gobierno-fotos**

El huracán María destruyó 70,000 viviendas en Puerto Rico **https://www.elnuevodia.com/noticias/locales/nota/elhuracanmariadestruyo 70000viviendasenpuertorico-2374555/**

El Huracán María provocó una catástrofe en el mercado laboral: **https://www.elnuevodia.com/negocios/economia/nota/elhuracanmaria provocounacatastrofeenelmercadolaboral-2374303/**

Week 3

Students continue their investigation through scaffolded activities. Teachers can model questions students might want to consider and provide examples of multimedia presentations they could use as ideas for their own presentations. We recommend using techniques that help students stay in the TL; when they become excited about the content, they can easily fall back to their L1 or the language of instruction the school uses. Examples of such techniques include giving roles, furnishing vocabulary, and providing a simple reporting format for different aspects of the preparation for the presentation to facilitate students' practice and promote the use of the TL (see also the MEEET approach introduced in Chapter 3). The use of the TL is also an explicit part of the rubric through which students are assessed by the teacher or their peers and/or assess themselves.

Groups are prompted to start articulating possible action plans—i.e., their potential actions as 'active citizens'—to address the consequences and challenges related to the aftermath of Hurricane Maria in their region or in Puerto Rico, depending on the questions they investigated (see Instructional Resource 3). Students also collaborate on the content, format and logistics of their presentation to the other groups. Depending on the group of students, teachers may decide to provide a format for them or leave it to their creativity in terms of how they want to present within certain given guidelines. We recommend a rubric explaining to students the aspects on which they will be assessed. For example, 'students should use simple language so that they speak freely (without reading from their slides).' Or: 'If students use slides, there should be minimal text but sufficient pictures supporting the text.'

In the work of this week, the Intercultural Competence skills of comparison and critical cultural awareness are further cultivated, as are interdisciplinary skills from mathematics—selecting solid quantitative data to support the rationale for potential action plans—and from social science: appreciating the role of culture in shaping their lives and society, as well as those of others. Intercultural Citizenship skills are also activated, specifically planning the mediation of an experience from elsewhere to their local region and the public.

Instructional Resources 3

These are suggested resources for further investigation, potential action plans, and presentations:

Articles from local media news

Federal information about preparation plans for hurricanes and other disasters, recovery assistance, and volunteer opportunities (currently available at): **https://www.fema.gov/es**

Spanish material from FEMA on preparation plans (currently available at): **https://www.fema.gov/media-library/assets/documents/93453**

Week 4

Students present their findings and ideas for potential action plans to other groups. Then they write reports to summarize what they have learned from each other. To achieve rich and meaningful learning from this activity, teachers must press for understanding of key issues surrounding the different aspects, e.g.: Do some aspects affect us more than others? How? Why? Students can be asked to keep an online journal and record their answers to questions as well as their own questions that come up during presentations.

Groups work on synthesizing the ideas that ensue from this deeper analysis of the findings and plans. (See Appendix 4.3 for focused chart for interpretation and comparison across groups to guide synthesis report.) Follow-up activities that help students compare the results and interpret and relate what they learn to their own contexts are important at this point. If possible, students should interact with community members with ties to Puerto Rico, or with a partner class in Puerto Rico, to receive additional perspectives and ask clarification questions so they can develop the skill of empathy, that is seeing the world from the other person's perspective—putting themselves 'in the other person's shoes' or (in the French version) *'dans la peau de l'autre'* ['in the other person's skin]. Reflection questions can include, *"Cuál fue la información más sorprendente que aprendiste de tus compañeros sobre Puerto Rico?"* ["What was the most surprising piece of information you learned from your partners in PR?"], *"Cuáles de las consecuencias del huracán crees que fueron las más difíciles para la gente?"* ["What consequences of Hurricane Maria do you think were most difficult for people?"].

Students would apply their Intercultural Competence attitudes, skills, and knowledge. For example, they would have to use the TL to interact and discover in real time new perspectives from their interlocutors, which in turn stimulates Intercultural Citizenship skills of interaction with the local community and their own perspectives. They would also apply their interdisciplinary skills of communicating mathematical and scientific ideas, as well as their social studies and English language arts skills of argumentation.

Week 5

The goal is to plan the final event. Through scaffolded activities, students prepare a list of action items that need to happen for the event. Then they divide the work and start inviting participants, reviewing the logistics, and advertising the event by preparing handouts, pamphlets, posters and/or a webpage. The teacher decides how much guidance students need. For example, some might benefit from a model for an invitation they modify, while others could work more independently.

Students must decide whether the event will be bilingual or two separate events, if the public is invited. If this is a school event, it is advisable to invite Spanish speaking community members to create a real communicative need for using the TL. Here it is crucial to help students use the TL meaningfully, lest they forget because they are so engaged in the task. The idea is actually to create situations in which they almost forget they are using the TL, to achieve authentic communicative and Intercultural Citizenship goals. The question we like to ask ourselves is: What resources and scaffolding can we provide that help students complete the tasks in the TL? For example, if students communicate with a community in the TL, they likely will want to learn how to make themselves understood in the TL. Another way to engage students in meaningful communication is to provide tasks rather than exercises or activities (VanPatten, 2017).

The activity this week is very much focused on Intercultural Citizenship, on acting in the community in the here and now.

Week 6

Students put the finishing touches on their presentations and finalize the event's details. The teacher reminds them of the rubric (that was either co-created or shared with the students). Then students present their findings and discuss action items, which could include fundraisers, letters to government representatives with inquiries or suggestions for actions, contacting organizations in the area or in Puerto Rico to collaborate on an action item, etc. They could also invite the school news club to take photos and write a report on the event. Local papers and/or a radio station could be invited, in which case the kind of scenario of immediate impact in the here and now presented in Chapter 1 becomes a reality, not just a role-play.

This culminating activity lets students apply and further develop their attitudes, skills and knowledge related to Intercultural Competence. They also use skills from other disciplines outside the classroom walls: skills of communicating mathematical and scientific ideas; argumentation skills from social studies and English language arts. This fosters the Intercultural Citizenship skills of introducing and mediating to the community new perspectives and potential actions on a phenomenon, which they have acquired through their classroom work and interactions with people in another country or with members from a different culture in their own community (possibly and preferably using their TL).

Table 4.2: Sample Unit Plan for Hurricane Maria Unit (adapted from Clementi & Terrill, 2017).

Language and Level / Grade	**Intermediate-level Spanish at High School** Approximate Length of Unit: 6 weeks Approximate Number of Minutes Weekly: 200
Theme/Topic	Natural Disasters: Hurricane Maria
Essential Question	What are the relationships between interdisciplinary knowledge of natural disasters and the quality of life in our interconnected contemporary world?
Unit Goals—Intercultural Citizenship	
What should learners know and be able to do by the end of the unit?	Learners will: ■ interpret and relate information about Hurricane Maria in specific regions in Puerto Rico to similar disasters in contemporary history; ■ discover and interact with others in the TL to gain new knowledge and perspectives on the issue at hand; ■ make judgments about how to deal with natural disasters based on specific evidence and different (cultural) perspectives (and understanding of their relationship with cultural products and practices); ■ present pertinent information to an outside audience, thus contribute to solving a problem in a local, national, or international community (action component) Learners will acquire knowledge about: ■ Hurricane Maria as an event of major societal as well as natural significance ■ how people respond to natural disasters, and how responses vary in different cultural contexts ■ how disasters are presented in the media, and how this varies across contexts

▶ ▶ ▶

Intercultural Citizenship Connections with Other Disciplines

Mathematics

- Analyze and interpret information using quantitative reasoning (reasoning that requires the use of mathematics in authentic situations, including socio-political, where estimation and knowledge from other disciplines might be crucial) to understand the phenomenon and support claims
- Use relative thinking to compare across data
- Create viable mathematical arguments drawn from evidence
- Use mathematical representations in meaningful ways to support argument
- Interpret and/or apply statistical data and representations in meaningful ways to support arguments

Science

- Construct an explanation based on valid and reliable evidence obtained from a variety of sources (including students' own investigations, models, theories, simulations, peer review) and the assumption that theories and laws that describe the natural world operate today as they did in the past and will continue to do so in the future. (NGSS: HS-ESS3-1)
- Design or refine a solution to a complex real-world problem, based on scientific knowledge, student-generated sources of evidence, prioritized criteria, and trade-off considerations. (NGSS: HS-ESS3-4)

Social Studies

- Understand how human beings create, learn, share, and adapt to culture
- Appreciate the role of culture in shaping their lives and society, as well as those of others
- Develop their perspectives of the world
- Understand where people, places, and resources are located and why they are there, and explore the relationship between human beings and the environment
- Understand the increasingly important and diverse global connections among world societies
- Learn about the rights and responsibilities of citizens of a democracy, and appreciate the importance of active citizenship

Other disciplines

- We focus on the three disciplines listed above, but strong connections can be drawn to specific standards in other disciplines, such as English Language Arts, Unified Arts, Geography, History, Political Science.

Summative Performance Tasks—Intercultural Citizenship

- These tasks let learners demonstrate how well they have met the unit's goals.
- The tasks follow the format of the IPA, but are integrated throughout the unit.
- The template encourages multiple interpretive tasks.
- The interpretive tasks inform the content of the presentational and interpersonal tasks.
- The tasks incorporate 21st-century skills.

Interpretive Mode

Read news articles on Hurricane Maria	Watch videos on Hurricane Maria	Analyze statistics on Hurricane Maria
Demonstrate understanding by completing a graphic organizer (See above list of Resources for suggestions)	Demonstrate understanding by synthesizing the information with the main points raised in the video (See above list of Resources for suggestions)	Demonstrate understanding by identifying the findings and evidence to incorporate in their presentation (See above list of Resources for suggestions)

Presentational Mode

- Work in groups to design multimedia presentation on the effects of Hurricane Maria on PR and the region
- On demand: Present individual findings to be included in presentations to the group (scaffolded through guided questions)
- Polished: Prepared and practiced presentation of results in town hall meeting

Interpersonal Mode

- Teacher moderates a meeting (of different classes or within the same class) in which students discuss what they have learned about Hurricane Maria as well as possible action projects based on their findings on the effects of Hurricane Maria
- Leading up to this assessment, we suggest the inclusion of an interpersonal assessment such as the following: students in groups of 2-3 discuss their key findings and how they want to present their recommendation to the whole group in a 'town hall' meeting format.)

Standards

Cultures (Sample Evidence)

Indicate the relationship between the product, practice, and perspective

Relating Cultural Practices and Products to Perspectives

Product: Hurricane Maria emergency housing and other products related to relief aid efforts

Practice: Discourse in the media coverage

Perspective: Analysis of the underlying values: acceptance of inevitability of natural disasters; value placed on human life and precaution

Connections (Sample Evidence)	Making Connections to Other Disciplines	Acquiring Information and Diverse Viewpoints
	For more detail, see above 'Inter-cultural Citizenship Connections with other Disciplines' ■ Mathematics ■ Sciences ■ Social Studies ■ English Language Arts ■ Arts	■ Differences in perspectives concerning disaster preparation in general and the effects of Hurricane Maria in specific ■ Importance of investigating multiple viewpoints using a variety of skills, attitudes, and knowledge from various disciplines
Comparisons (Sample Evidence)	Language Comparisons	Cultural Comparisons
	Analysis and use of terms in English and Spanish, e.g., whether 'safety' and 'security' have equivalent terms and the same connotations	Analysis of disaster preparation in Puerto Rico and the US (see Intercultural Citizenship Goals)
Communities (Sample Evidence)	School and Global Communities	Lifelong Learning
	■ Engagement with community in investigation of status quo of effects of Hurricane Maria ■ Presentation to local community analysis of comparable practices of disaster preparation in e.g., Mexico	Learners take the role of teachers in educating their local community

Connections to Common Core and/or other required standards	21st century standards: collaboration 21st century standards: creativity 21st century standards: critical thinking **Common Core ELA Standards for Reading** ■ Key Ideas and Details: CCSS.ELA-Literacy.RI.9-10.1, CCSS.ELA-LITERACY.RI.11-12.1. ■ Integration of knowledge and ideas: CCSS.ELA-LITERACY.RI.9-10.7, ■ CCSS.ELA-LITERACY.RI.9-10.8, CCSS.ELA-LITERACY.RI.11-12.7. ■ Range of Reading and Level of Text Complexity: CCSS.ELA-LITERACY.RI.9-10.10, CCSS.ELA-LITERACY.RI.11-12.10, **Common Core ELA Standards for Writing** ■ Text Types and Purposes: CCSS.ELA-LITERACY.W.9-10.1, CCSS.ELA-LITERACY.W.9-10.2, CCSS.ELA-LITERACY.W.9-10.3.A, CCSS.ELA-LITERACY.W.9-10.3.E, CCSS.ELA-LITERACY.W.11-12.1, CCSS.ELA-LITERACY.W.11-12.2, CCSS.ELA-LITERACY.W.11-12.3.A, CCSS.ELA-LITERACY.W.11-12.3.E. ▶▶▶

Connections to Common Core and/or other required standards *— continued*	**Common Core ELA Standards for Writing** — *continued* ■ Production and Distribution of Writing: CCSS.ELA-LITERACY.W.9-10.4, CCSS.ELA-LITERACY.W.9-10.6, CCSS.ELA-LITERACY.W.11-12.4, CCSS.ELA-LITERACY.W.11-12.6. ■ Research to Build and Present Knowledge: CCSS.ELA-LITERACY.W.9-10.7, CCSS.ELA-LITERACY.W.9-10.8, CCSS.ELA-LITERACY.W.9-10.9.B, CCSS.ELA-LITERACY.W.11-12.7, CCSS.ELA-LITERACY.W.11-12.8, ■ Range of Writing: CCSS.ELA-LITERACY.W.9-10.10, ■ CCSS.ELA-LITERACY.W.11-12.10. **Common Core Standards for Mathematical Practice** ■ CCSS.MATH.PRACTICE.MP1, CCSS.MATH.PRACTICE.MP2, CCSS.MATH.PRACTICE.MP3, CCSS.MATH.PRACTICE.MP4, CCSS.MATH.PRACTICE.MP5, CCSS.MATH.PRACTICE.MP6, CCSS.MATH.PRACTICE.MP7, CCSS.MATH.PRACTICE.MP8. **Next Generation Science Standards** ■ NGSS: HS-ESS3-1, NGSS: HS-ESS3-4 **National Curriculum Standards for Social Studies** ■ THEME 1, THEME 3, THEME 9, THEME 10. *Elaborated descriptions appear under connections to other disciplines above,*

Toolbox

Can-Do Statements

Interpretive	■ I can demonstrate my understanding of the impact of Hurricane Maria on different areas of concern for Puerto Rico, other countries, the U.S., and my own community. ■ I can interpret information about the different ways in which Hurricane Maria has impacted other countries, the U.S., and my own community. ■ I can analyze different sources of information to better understand the effects of Hurricane Maria.
Presentational	■ I can describe experiences and events related to Hurricane Maria using a range of conduits: visual and/or oral presentations. ■ I can make others aware of the impact of Hurricane Maria on PR and my community. ■ I can express and support recommendations for disaster preparation and recovery efforts in my and in my partners' community.
Interpersonal	■ I can ask and answer questions about natural disasters. ■ I can discuss action items to address effects of Hurricane Maria.

▶ ▶ ▶

Language Functions	Related Structures / Patterns	Priority Vocabulary
Define and describe different aspects of the effects of Hurricane Maria (HM)	El huracán María fué un huracán de cuarta categoría con vientos que alcanzaron una velocidad de...	valores numéricos (numbers) valores relativos (relative values)
Compare and contrast effects of HM	María afectó un área más grande que la afectada por huracán Harvey en Texas pero menos que la zona afectada por...	comparaciones (comparisons) porcentajes (percentages) incremento/disminución (increase/decrease)
Analyze numbers related to HM	Los porcentajes de mortalidad ocasionados por María en Puerto Rico sobrepasan los valores de...	estadísticas (statistics) gráfico circular (pie chart) gráfico de barras (bar graph)
Evaluate possible action items related to addressing the effects of HM	Proponemos preparar a nuestra comunidad para la potencial inmigración de gente necesitada haciendo....	velocidad de cambio (rate of change) diferencia (differences)
Interpret written text and oral information about natural disasters and HM	Cuando las noticias hablan del impacto en la salud que María tuvo, se refieren a...	impacto social (social impact) impacto económico (economic impact)
Summarize important facts about the effects of HM	Podemos resumir estos datos de la siguiente forma...	clases sociales/económicas (social/economic classes)
Ask and answer questions about action items addressing effects of HM	Cuál fue el índice de mortalidad del huracán?	derechos humanos (human rights)
Express invitation to community members to attend the Community Event.	Invitamos a los miembros de nuestro pueblo a participar de...	
Negotiate the content and design of presentations (for the event as well as for informal presentations in the classroom)	Es mejor usar un gráfico de barras para mostrar...	
Report and present results in Community Event	Nuestro grupo investigó el impacto del Huracán María en el área...	

▶ ▶ ▶

Key Learning Activities/Formative Assessments

This is a representative sample of activities/assessments across the 3 modes of communication.

Learning Activity/ Formative Assessment *(Sample activities are listed from the beginning to the end of the unit.)*	How does this activity support the unit goals or performance tasks?	Mode of Communication
Exploration of disasters in one area (Video, interviews)	■ Students acquire the knowledge related to natural disasters in general, and Hurricane Maria in specific. ■ Exposure to various perspectives (open-mindedness, tolerance of ambiguity) ■ Students interpret information from another culture and relate it to their own	interpretive (and interpersonal and presentational if done in group work)
Preparation of presentation of assigned/chosen natural disaster to other groups	■ Students analyze (using language, mathematics, social studies knowledge and skills), mediate, discover and interact	interpretive, interpersonal, presentational
Presentation of assigned/ chosen natural disaster to the groups	■ Students learn important presentation and communication skills	presentational, in Q&A: interpersonal
Synthesize findings of different groups (using specific format)	■ Critical cultural awareness	interpretive, interpersonal, presentational
Exploration of one aspect of effects of Hurricane Maria on Puerto Rico and the US (This includes interpretation of written materials, such as new articles and testimonies, as well as visual, written, and oral information in videos and information gained through interaction with witnesses and people with personal connections to HM and to Puerto Rico)	■ Knowledge related to one type of impact of Hurricane Maria on Puerto Rico and the US in general and the students' region in particular ■ Exposure to various perspectives (open-mindedness, tolerance of ambiguity) ■ Interpret information from another culture and relate to their own	interpretive, interpersonal, presentational

▶▶▶

Preparation of presentation of assigned/chosen aspect to other groups	■ Students analyze (using language, mathematics, social studies knowledge and skills), mediate, discover and interact,	interpretive, interpersonal, presentational
Presentation of assigned/ chosen aspects to the groups	■ Students learn important presentation and communication skills	interpersonal, presentational
Plan Community Event (invitations, advertising, logistics)	■ Students learn important skills for reaching out to the community and different ways in which to attract different audiences	interpretive, interpersonal, presentational
Community Event: Presentation of findings	■ Students learn important presentation and communication skills to address an audience outside of the classroom environment and to argue for their proposed action plans	presentational (and interpersonal in Q&A)
Community Event: Discussion of action items	■ Mediate between different members of the audience; help present and synthesize the meaning of suggestions made by the audience and by classmates; apply critical cultural awareness to judge events based on specific criteria. ■ This represents an action item for Intercultural Citizenship and at the same time creates opportunities for additional Intercultural Citizenship through projects that follow up on this discussion.	interpersonal

▶▶▶

Resources	Technology Integration
■ Resources to reactivate and introduce vocabulary related to natural disasters: a Quizlet set of vocabulary for natural disasters: (https://quizlet.com/18508325/spanish-natural-disasters-vocab-flash-cards/) or an online slideshow with vocabulary (https://study.com/academy/lesson/spanish-terms-for-natural-disasters-emergencies.html) ■ Resources for pre-assessment: Video images of the aftermath of Hurricane Maria https://www.youtube.com/watch?v=wfxPGrXj-sE ■ Resources with general information about natural disasters in Spanish to guide the group work: http://www.geoenciclopedia.com/desastres-naturales/ ■ See also Appendix 4.2: Activity and guiding questions for group work ■ News article showcasing Hurricane Maria in numbers and pictures https://www.univision.com/puerto-rico/wlii/noticias/huracan-maria/en-numeros-oficiales-y-fotos-asi-va-la-recuperacion-de-puerto-rico-a-un-mes-de-maria-segun-el-gobierno-fotos ■ Impact of Hurricane Maria on housing: https://www.elnuevodia.com/noticias/locales/nota/elhuracanmariadestruyo70000viviendasenpuertorico-2374555/ ■ Effects of Hurricane Maria on labor market: https://www.elnuevodia.com/negocios/economia/nota/elhuracanmariaprovocounacatastrofeenelmercadolaboral-2374303/ ■ Video in Spanish illustrating/modelling how to use the data in meaningful ways: https://www.youtube.com/watch?v=hhUvtP-hOgQ ■ Federal information about preparation plans for hurricanes and other disasters, recovery assistance, and volunteer opportunities: https://www.fema.gov/es ■ Spanish material from FEMA on preparation plans: https://www.fema.gov/media-library/assets/documents/93453	

Community	
■ participate in efforts to handle the effects of a natural disaster in our own community	■ understand the effects that a natural disaster locally or elsewhere has in their own community: immigration, economical, health, energy resources, human resources
■ participate in efforts to improve preparation plans based on lessons learned from the impact of recent disasters in the community and in other countries	■ analyze existing preparation plans
	raise awareness of the impact disasters have in own community

Unit Template adapted from Keys to Planning for Learning (Clementi & Terrill, 2017)

Conclusion

In Chapter 4 we have taken you through a detailed process of planning that integrates work in several subjects with the main focus on languages. We have described weekly language classroom activities that help students develop and apply the knowledge, attitudes and skills that are part of Intercultural Communicative Competence and apply them in the here and now as Intercultural Citizens in a context that is meaningful to them as well as their immediate or the global community. Most language units are suitable for the incorporation of Intercultural Citizenship as illustrated in this chapter, and many connections to fundamental content from other subject areas can help enrich the learning experience of students, and their education in general.

We encourage you to look into other units of your class curriculum and use the example and activities detailed in this chapter, along with the questions we have posed, to help you develop your own units for Intercultural Citizenship and bring your ideas to colleagues in other subjects to create interdisciplinary and integrated learning opportunities for your students. We know from experience that students need our help understanding the myriad of connections that can be made between subjects in order to understand problems that affect their community and the world. They also need our help to work collaboratively to understand how different perspectives, practices, and cultures can help shape plausible solutions. In this chapter we have shown an example of the significant impact language education can have in this endeavor.

Now, in Chapter 5, we shall investigate with you the rationale for this kind of teaching, why it is important to teach languages for interdisciplinary Intercultural Citizenship—a crucial issue in how education systems need to respond to changing societal conditions and go beyond the disciplinary divisions of traditional curricula. There are implications for all interdisciplinary work and for educators' professional identities; this also applies to the effects of interdisciplinary cooperation on language educators' views of themselves and their work.

Why teach languages for interdisciplinary Intercultural Citizenship
—THE BIGGER PICTURE

To compete in today's global society, today's students must be proficient communicators, creators, critical thinkers, and collaborators (the "Four Cs"). To do so, students must master additional subject areas, including foreign languages, the arts, geography, science, and social studies. Educators must complement all of those subjects with the "Four Cs" to prepare young people for citizenship and the global workforce (National Education Association, 2012, p. 5).

In this chapter, we provide a rationale for teaching interdisciplinary Intercultural Citizenship. We show that this way of teaching offers an excellent opportunity to prepare students for the challenges they face individually and we face as a society. This is supported by cutting edge research in language teaching and learning as well as other educational disciplines.

We also show why language educators are perfectly situated to collaborate with colleagues to prepare students to solve real world problems as intercultural citizens and how this helps them become advocates for all language learners.

Finally, we explain how this approach requires a reconceptualization of professional identities.

The quote above provides a good overview of our purpose in this book: that our students must be prepared to integrate what they learn, both in the different subject areas and outside of school, to make sense of the complexities of the world they live in. They must be good communicators and collaborators in the search for creative solutions to increasingly global and interconnected problems they face in their current and future lives. This is best done through interdisciplinary work. In this chapter, we want to discuss with you the wider, deeper significance of our approach, and to develop further the concept of and rationale for interdisciplinary language teaching as a means of contextualizing the suggestions we have made in previous chapters.

Every educator must advocate for an interdisciplinary education. No subject area can remain in isolation; when learners apply their learning, it is rarely done in the silos of separated subject areas. In this chapter, we provide the resources that might help you in advocacy efforts, including some longer quotes and links to the sources or references to facilitate your access to the complete papers.

We are sure you agree that language education is crucial in the educational mission to prepare our students to thrive in today's world and contribute to society in meaningful, constructive ways. We have often found that point of view when talking to and working with teachers, though we have also found that they sometimes lack the confidence and resources to make this argument for other educationists or for stakeholders in society in general. Mike, one of our authors, had this experience as Head of Languages in a secondary school, when the headteacher wanted to cut language teaching because it was not useful or popular; he had to produce a paper to defend languages, especially the second foreign language, in the curriculum. Manuela also observes that language programs are often some of the first on the chopping block, either when teachers retire or during budgetary crises.

We urge you to confidently find your voice to promote this crucial endeavor, for we are convinced that, in advocating for Intercultural Citizenship education, we actively contribute to a better understanding of the crucial role language education plays in our students' lives and in our society.

To present our ideas, arguments and resources, we ask the following:

1. Why must language education get involved in the world, and draw on citizenship education to do so?
2. Why must we engage in interdisciplinary work to teach languages for Intercultural Citizenship?
3. How is teaching languages for interdisciplinary Intercultural Citizenship supported by current research in language teaching and learning?
4. How can this approach help educators in their advocacy for all language learners and for languages for all?
5. How does this approach relate to our professional identities?

The practical outcomes of this chapter you can use include:

- the development of a rationale for language education regarding its relevance to solving the challenges we face in society today;
- the development of a rationale for language education regarding its relevance to the general educational mission;
- ideas and arguments for preparing advocacy for teaching languages for interdisciplinary Intercultural Citizenship.

1. Why must language education get involved in the world, and draw on citizenship education to do so?

To go back to the question raised by Moeller & Abbott (2018, p. 21), "How exactly does one go about making the vision of languages as a core subject for all learners a reality?", our view is that one significant contribution to answering it comes through teaching languages for Intercultural Citizenship. By the end of the chapter, we hope you will clarify your views about the indispensability of language education and its necessity for our students to understand the world and act in it meaningfully. We also hope to have helped you articulate and advocate for your views in your own individualized way to match your specific context.

In the White Paper "Languages for All? A Final Report," Abbott et al. (2014, p. 4) discuss their vision of language education in predominantly English-speaking countries and then focus on the U.S., for which this access to language education would comprise a full range of abilities:

- appreciation of the role of language and culture in contemporary domestic and international societies;
- usable skills for domestic interaction and international travel;
- high-level skills enabling global professional practice;
- expertise providing language education and language technologies.

Pause to Ponder

1. How can (language) education for Intercultural Citizenship contribute to the vision stated by Abbott et al. above?
2. How do you think we can contribute to "making the vision of language as a core subject for all learners a reality" by teaching languages for interdisciplinary Intercultural Citizenship?
3. If you were asked how language teaching contributes to the general educational mission of preparing our students for the demands of today's world, what would be the three most important points you would mention?
4. Are the factors you mentioned helpful in strengthening the position of languages as a core subject? If yes, can you explain this to somebody who is not in language education?

Larsen-Freeman (2018) summarized the challenge of the times we live in, as well as the opportunities for language education, as follows:

> The Zeitgeist is one of rapid change and turmoil, and none of us can be immune to the natural and political threats or social injustices it presents. In a more salutary light, the compression of time and space that technology

affords, the opportunities for international travel and careers in a global society, and the chances for ordinary citizens to lead transnational lives have made the advantages of knowing another language more apparent (pp. 58-59).

Let us first consider the role of language in helping our students survive and strive in today's world. Our students face natural, economic, and political challenges that seem bigger and more complex than ever before. This is further complicated, as Lynch et al. (n.d.) point out, by lack of agreement and difficulty in finding common solutions (https://humilityandconviction.uconn.edu/blank/what-is-intellectual-humility/): "One thing we all seem to agree on is that, increasingly, we don't agree on very much. Fundamental and extremely divisive disagreement over religion, morality and science is pervasive in our culture" (p. 1). As a first step in searching for any agreement, we must be able to take someone else's viewpoint—to 'decenter'—which is a fundamental purpose of language teaching and learning. The problem has been how to realize this purpose in practice, but new developments in teaching Intercultural Communicative Competence can help us make this a reality.

Lynch et al. (n.d.) argue that, to reach or at least approach agreement, intellectual humility and conviction are crucial for meaningful dialogue, and there are important connections between learning a language, especially developing Intercultural Citizenship skills and attitudes, and Intellectual Humility (Wagner, Cardetti, & Byram, 2018). The research on Intellectual Humility helps us to review and refine what we mean by 'decentering' and understanding the cultures of other social groups, and intellectual humility is important in all dialogue dealing with environmental dangers, political turmoil, economic crisis and other complex, urgent challenges. Important international organizations have long planned educational and other initiatives to address these challenges. The interdisciplinary research and engagement project Humility and Conviction in Public Life (HCPL) at the University of Connecticut investigates the role of Intellectual Humility in addressing the need for constructive dialogue. The Council of Europe (2018, Volume 1) has created a *Reference Framework of Competences for Democratic Culture* through which "young people acquire the knowledge, values and capacity to be responsible citizens in modern, divers, democratic societies" (p. 5).

We lack a clear focus and understanding of common goals in citizenship education, and the *Reference Framework of Competences for Democratic Culture* (2018) has been designed to bridge that gap, partly in response to political developments in Europe. In his foreword to the document, Secretary General Jagland argues, "The need for it was brought into sharp focus by the many terrorist attacks across Europe in recent years. Education is a medium- to long-term investment in preventing violent extremism and radicalization, but the work must start now" (p. 5). The document is being propagated through a network of advisors throughout Europe and with a project to create a portfolio for the documentation and assessment of 'competences for democratic culture.'

This brings us to the second part of Larsen-Freeman's statement above: the types of challenges we face increase the need for mediators who can communicate with those of different opinions and/or mediate between those who speak different languages and have different backgrounds. This mediation skill has been prioritized in the European approach to language teaching. In the new *Companion Volume to the Common European Framework of Reference for Languages* (2018), definitions and indicators for the skill of mediation help teachers to include mediation in their teaching objectives.

So we need language education more than ever, which offers a tremendous opportunity for our profession. In 2017 the Commission on Language Learning authored the report *America's Languages: Investing in Language Education for the 21st Century* in response to a request from members of the U.S. Senate and House of Representatives to consider certain questions:

> How does language learning influence economic growth, cultural diplomacy, the productivity of future generations, and the fulfillment of all Americans? What actions should the nation take to ensure excellence in all languages as well as international education and research, including how we may more effectively use current resources to advance language learning?" (American Academy of Arts and Sciences, 2017, p. v).

Key findings of the report include:

> The ability to understand, speak, read, and write in world languages, in addition to English, is critical to success in business, research, and international relations in the twenty-first century.

> The U.S. needs more people to speak languages other than English in order to provide social and legal services for a changing population.

> The study of a second language has been linked to improved learning outcomes in other subjects, enhanced cognitive ability, and the development of empathy and effective interpretive skills. The use of a second language has been linked to a delay in certain manifestations of aging.

> The U.S. lags behind most nations of the world, including European nations and China, in the percentage of its citizens who have some knowledge of a second language. (American Academy of Arts and Sciences, 2017, p. viii).

The Commission on Language Learning (American Academy of Arts and Sciences, 2017) therefore recommends:

> ... a national strategy to improve access to as many languages as possible for people of every region, ethnicity, and socioeconomic background—that is, to value language education as a persistent national need similar to education in math or English, and to ensure that a useful level of proficiency is within every student's reach (p. viii).

1. What is your immediate reaction to these findings and recommendations?

2. Was there anything you found surprising?

3. How can the information above be useful in your advocacy for language educa-tion? Think about different groups of stakeholders (e.g., students who are studying languages, students who decide to opt out of languages, colleagues in your institu-tion, administrators, parents, politicians, community members, etc.) and what the arguments you would share would be for each group.

As we shall see below, there now seems to be common acceptance in the United States that its citizens must be equipped with language skills and Intercultural Competence. Research indicates that Americans believe students must learn languages. Approximately 70% of respondents to a survey conducted by Rivers et al. (2013) valued languages as much as math and science in education (Rivers, Robinson, Harwood & Brecht, 2013). Unfortunately, this belief is not yet manifested in sufficient material support.

ACTFL promotes language education for all learners, based on a clear understanding that language education entails preparing students for world readiness *(World-Readiness Standards for Learning Languages)* and communication and relationship creation with people from other cultures *(NCSSFL-ACTFL Can-Do Statements for Intercultural Communication)*. The "Languages for All" Report also emphasized the "value proposition" of language:

> This vision has to be expressed within a consistent and convincing message about the "value proposition" of language, both to the individual and the broader society as well as about the feasibility of access and effectiveness of the learning process. The direct value of a language competent citizenry to a multilingual society includes both international (military/political, economic, and social)—all well documented—as well as domestic (government and private sector products and services). The Value Proposition for individuals can run from the immediately pragmatic—jobs and higher pay—to general education (cognitive advantages of bilingualism, literacy), to broader access to global information, resources, and people, innovative products and services (that more and more come from abroad), and finally to the most "esoteric" (well-rounded education). The advantages to society in the political/military, economic (GDP), and social spheres must be documented with real evidence, so too the advan-tages for individuals (e.g., lifelong earning power). (Abbott et al., 2014, p. 6)

The values are placed on a continuum from the 'pragmatic' to the 'esoteric,' which implies they are all equally important, but we believe the 'esoteric' is the overarching rationale. It is called 'esoteric' perhaps because, unlike easily understood concrete evidence (e.g., jobs and higher pay), the rationale for well-rounded education is more abstract. We must thus articulate this rationale in persuasive ways, supported by concrete evidence and emphasizing the satisfactions of a well-rounded education and its contribution to the whole life of the individual and society, the life of the mind and spirit, economic life and material well-being.

The argument starts with students themselves, who can then pass on their experience and convictions to others. We must help our students to reflect on and see that (a) they are able to apply languages in context, (b) they understand the role of languages and cultures in their lives and the lives of others, and (c) they develop the knowledge, skills, and attitudes contributing to their growing Intercultural Competence and their abilities to use this in society and for social change. We will come back to the first two points and continue here with the third, since we can also find clarity and evidence for this in the literature.

A number of organizations understand that language education must include the development of Intercultural Competence or global citizenship. An example is the Programme for International Student Assessment (PISA) testing program by the Organisation for Economic Co-operation and Development (OECD):

> The OECD PISA framework defines global competence as: "the capacity to examine local, global, and intercultural issues, to *understand and appreciate* the perspectives and world views of others, to engage in open, appropriate and effective *interactions* with people from different cultures, and to act for collective well-being and sustainable development" (Bayer, 2017—emphasis added).

The PISA documents present clear evidence that educationists view citizenship skills as crucial to personal development in a competitive world. Whether or not countries decide to compare their students with those in other countries, as the OECD suggests, the focus on citizenship cannot be ignored. It will be an element of all teaching—we discuss the interdisciplinary approach in the next section—and is already part of what some language teachers believe is the way forward.

Pause to Ponder

1. How are global competencies described in the quote above?
2. If you take Byram's (2008) Model of Intercultural Citizenship explained in Chapter 2, which components (knowledge, skills of interpreting and relating, skills of discovery and interaction, attitudes, mediation, critical cultural awareness, action in the community) do you think address the aspects mentioned in the description above?

So far, we have shared arguments for a need for students to learn languages to participate meaningfully in today's society. We have also argued for enabling our students to use what they learn in language education to solve social problems in the here and now rather than make assumptions about future usefulness of language education. This connects (world) language education with today's world, and language teachers should be able to explain how the link with citizenship education creates an enrichment of language teaching, above all because of the ways in which it has developed a systematic, well-founded methodology for linking learning in school to action in the community.

We now move on to the next question which concerns leveraging opportunities of language education to foster collaborations with other subjects.

2. Why must we engage in interdisciplinary work to teach languages for Intercultural Citizenship?

The information provided so far convinces us that language education *must* play a crucial role in our students' education and in their lives. Yet, even after extended foreign language study, students often fail to (1) develop advanced foreign language proficiency and (2) see the relevance of language study in their immediate lives, especially in English-speaking countries, as a survey of young people in the United Kingdom indicates (Young, 2014). Although there may be many reasons for this—motivations, perceptions in society of the (lack of) importance of language learning, inadequate policies and facilities in schools and universities—our students must learn Intercultural Citizenship skills and learn to think critically about the world in which they live.

Although our students are not always aware of it, language(s) and cultures are very much part of their lives. Knowing how their identity is shaped by languages and cultures plays a crucial role for their well-being. Understanding how languages and cultures influence the lives of others helps them in their critical evaluation of many problems we face (e.g., refugee "crisis"). As language educators, we must help our students see the value of all cultures and the value of their diverse heritage and backgrounds. We must encourage them to actively shape their curricula and the kinds of questions they want to ask (Clementi & Terrill, 2017).

> **We must ask our students to bring all of their knowledge, skills and experiences from other subjects and their lives outside of school to our classrooms.**

From this starting point, we can broaden students' awareness of how skills and knowledge in other disciplines are not separate and should not be kept separated by the way in which curricula are organized by discipline. We must ask our students to bring all of their knowledge, skills and experiences from other subjects and their lives outside of school to our classrooms and make sense of the many connections they can make with what they learn in language classes, and vice versa. This means leaving out of our curricula anything irrelevant to our students' lives. Such a way of teaching requires flexibility on our part; we need to be aware of what is going on in our students' lives to make sound judgments concerning the relevance of topics for them. This will require us to investigate topics in which we have less expertise.

1. Do teachers need to be the experts of the topics they teach? If not, what are some strategies that can help them plan successful lessons without feeling that they need to have all the answers?
2. What are some ways in which language teachers can approach teaching topics that they feel less knowledgeable about?
3. Do teachers need to re-think their professional identity and what their purpose is? Do they need to expand their purpose to include matters of social justice, for example?

Interdisciplinarity comes into play here. If our mission in language education is to help our students face the challenges of today's world, we must enable them to interact with these challenges. While some challenges might be linguistic in nature, hence more likely part of our expertise, most will be complex and require some knowledge and skills from a variety of disciplines, as Blodget (2017) implies:

> As the problems we face become increasingly complex and interrelated, not to mention deadly, the need to eliminate borders becomes more urgent. Providing occasional interdisciplinary experiences is not enough. Students need to experience borderless education as the norm—every year they are in school. Educators need to imagine new ways to structure borderless schools and to model borderless learning. (p. 8)

Complex problems do require interdisciplinary approaches: "What is considered interdisciplinary today might be considered disciplinary tomorrow" (National Science Foundation, n.d.). This indicates that researchers and teachers must deal with fuzzy, rapidly changing boundaries among diverse disciplines. We language teachers must be open to this interdisciplinarity, even at the risk of exposing ourselves to uncertainty. After all, we talk about tolerance of ambiguity as an important skill in Intercultural Competence. This gives us an opportunity to practice just that.

In Intellectual Humility, our acknowledgment and taking ownership of our 'weaknesses,' of not being experts in everything, is key (Whitcomb, Battaly, Baehr, & Howard-Snyder, 2017), since evaluation of our knowledge and skills in certain areas can help us practice and develop our own as well as our students' Intellectual Humility. We must also acknowledge any fear or doubt we may have. We therefore ask you pause and ponder the following.

In answering the first of our questions for this chapter, we have expressed a certain philosophy of language education. We have talked about the educational value of language learning which goes beyond the focus on material gains, which also come with language learning. We have now also contextualized language teaching with other subjects/disciplines.

1. How does this philosophy of language education resonate with you? Perhaps you have had anecdotal experiences which are examples of the educational value?
2. If you think about potential collaborations with teachers of other subjects, how would you describe this philosophy and explain it to a non-linguist?
3. Are there parts of this philosophy and way of teaching you find problematic or unrealistic?
4. In what ways does your way of teaching match what was suggested here?
5. Are there aspects you do not implement/address yet, but you think would be a good idea to?

However, Blodget (2017) also points out that interdisciplinary collaboration is far from being the norm in education: "Despite decades of talk about interdisciplinary courses, despite the focus on STEM and STEAM, it remains monumentally difficult to get these departments to work together—even those with the most obvious relationships, such as math and science, English and foreign languages, or the arts and any other department" (p. 2).

Interdisciplinarity and STEM. If you have attended conferences on world languages teaching over the past years, you will likely have observed the growing interest in STEM (Science, Technology, Engineering and Mathematics) as well as STEAM (Science, Technology, Engineering, Art and Mathematics) reflected in a number of presentations, workshops, and publications. Some see this as a threat to the Humanities, while others consider it an opportunity to develop and showcase relationships between the disciplines. STEM proponents at times welcome the addition and connection with art, literacy, and languages in STEAM, while others fear a "watering down" of the STEM subjects. It is not our goal in this publication to rate the importance of various contributions of different disciplines, but to argue for a more holistic view that lets our students see the value of all education in their lives. As such, we welcome conversations about how we can collaborate to help our students meaningfully connect what they learn in different subjects/disciplines and relate it to the everyday world.

Indeed, the STEAM movement evolved from the acknowledgment that many discoveries and advances had resulted from drawing upon the STEM disciplines and the arts (Root-Bernstein and Root-Bernstein, 1999), as well as artists' many contributions to scientific and technological breakthroughs (e.g., sculptor Patricia Billings invented 'geobond' while trying to improve plaster, and artists Heather Ackroyd and Dan Harvey revolutionized plant nutrient screening through painting). There was also support for the STEAM movement from neuroeducation researchers who reported "tight correlations between arts training and improvements in cognition, attention, and learning" (Hardiman, Magsamen, McKhann, & Eilber, 2009, p. 23). STEAM education proponents also argue that exposure to the arts could demonstrate to students in STEM fields the societal, economic and political implications of scientific discovery and technological development (Grasso & Burkins, 2010). STEAM initiatives can be found across all educational levels and in many different formats.

Successful college-level combinations of STEM with arts and humanities include the Center of Interdisciplinary Science for Art, Architecture, and Archaeology at the University of California, San Diego, which focuses on engineering and adapting technology toward fulfilling the needs for cultural heritage diagnostics (an emerging field of archaeology) such as multi-dimensional and multi-spectral surveying. Also, the Digital Sound and Music project originated from a grant through the National Science Foundation to draw more students to the study of computer science by connecting them with art and digital sound production. The project has since evolved into a body of curricular material for computer science teachers and students that incorporates music, audio, and the performing arts (Shen, Jiang, & Liu, 2015).

The National Academies of Sciences, Engineering, and Medicine (2018) support interdisciplinary endeavors. When discussing higher education's chief challenges and opportunities, they emphasize:

> ...[t]he need to cultivate more robust cultural and ethical commitments to empathy, inclusion, and respect for the rich diversity of human identity and experience. Truly robust knowledge depends on the capacity to recognize the critical limitations of particular ways of knowing, to achieve the social relations appropriate to an inclusive and democratic society, and to cultivate due humility. These commitments are as essential to productive professional environments as they are to wider civic life. They are also critical to creating shared aspirations of the futures we want and to cultivating the forms of inquiry, innovation, and creative expression that will help build those futures. (p. 55)

Thus, the call for interdisciplinary work that supports Intercultural Citizenship education is well articulated and growing.

Pause to Ponder

1. What do you think are some reasons why colleagues from different disciplines find it hard to collaborate?
2. Can you think of some solutions for the challenges you identified?

Since language education has a prominent role to play in Intercultural Citizenship education, the success of these interdisciplinary efforts depends upon the engagement of language education in our curricula. Some universities successfully integrate language education with other subjects such as engineering in the form of dual degree programs. Often called Cultures and Languages Across the Curriculum (CLAC), these programs combine cultures and languages with another subject according to the natural connection between the disciplines (see https://clacconsortium.org/ for more information). For example, certain engineering topics are studied and developed foremost in German-speaking contexts (certain car models, some green technology, etc.), so the ability to access information about the subject and especially to interact with German-speaking colleagues in their language provides numerous Intercultural Citizenship opportunities for students.

After all, interaction with others is not simply a matter of the formal discussions of seminars and workshops, where English is undeniably often present. In one debate about the value of teaching languages in English-speaking countries reported in the English newspaper *The Guardian*, one of its pundits, Simon Jenkins, argued that language learning is not necessary and there are always other ways to understand other countries. Jenkins' view is refuted by a well-known academic, Mary Beard (2017), with panache:

> Even where in Europe the *lingua franca* of (academic) papers is English, I can promise you that the language of the bar isn't (or the toilets, for that matter). You get left out of an awful lot of what is really going on if you can only communicate in English. (p. 6)

Furthermore, English speakers may not be aware of the efforts others are making to speak in their second or third or even fourth foreign language, thus dominating conversations thoughtlessly, which leads to resentment and even rejection of what they are saying. For instance, North America has a growing group of students who speak languages other than English as part of their family life and experiences. In many courses of study and professions, students likely benefit from speaking the language of heritage language communities. Combining a discipline with language proficiency makes 'pragmatic' sense so students can understand their immediate surroundings, but also adds to the 'esoteric' value of a rounded education. Thus an entire community's willingness to access its various languages becomes key to the success of interdisciplinary education, as well as a matter of social justice language teachers can address.

In short, as we teach our students what they can use in their lives, we connect STEM with the humanities, and both scientific and educational communities agree that this cooperation with other disciplines can and should broaden. We now turn to a discussion of complex problem-solving, a richer form of interdisciplinarity which is often part of Intercultural Citizenship education.

Complex problem-solving. To learn languages for Intercultural Citizenship, students must be prepared to solve complex problems. Beghetto (2018) discusses the need for this preparation but also introduces some of the complexities involved, referring in particular to 'agentic engagement':

Given that a fundamental goal of school is to prepare young people for the unknowable future, it makes sense that students should learn how to respond to uncertainty. Providing students with opportunities to learn how to respond productively to uncertainty will help prepare them for the kinds of real-world challenges they face now and will face in the future. Routine assignments fall short in this regard because they are designed to remove uncertainty, not insert it (Getzels, 1964). Further, such tasks offer limited opportunities for student initiative, or what motivational researchers call agentic engagement (Cheon & Reeve, 2015; Reeve & Tseng, 2011). Agentic engagement refers to students proactively contributing to their own learning and instruction by, for instance, identifying problems they want to solve and coming up with their own ways of solving them. Not much of what students learn and do in school relates to actual problem-solving. If you already know how to move from A to Z, then you don't have a problem; you have an exercise (Robertson, 2017) or, at best, a "pseudo-problem" (Getzels, 1964). A problem is not a problem unless it involves some level of uncertainty. The more uncertainty, the more complex the problem. It may seem as if we are caught between two opposing aims. On the one hand, routine tasks play an important role in helping students learn academic subject matter, but they don't provide opportunities to engage with uncertainty. On the other hand, real problems encourage students to deal with the unknown, but we can't simply throw our students into the deep waters of complex challenges and hope that they will somehow learn to swim by themselves. (p. 2)

Pause to Ponder

1. How do you view the tension between providing students with "real and complex problems" and "routine assignments"?
2. Do you think we can expect students to make sense of what they learn in different subjects and apply their knowledge and skills later in life, or do you think we must help them start finding solutions to complex problems now?
3. What is the role of interdisciplinary Intercultural Citizenship education in this educational mission?
4. If you think back to the examples in earlier chapters, how do students have agentic engagement in Intercultural Citizenship projects?

As language teachers, we may not have noticed Beghetto's (2018) distinction between safety of routine tasks and the uncertainty of problem-solving, because much of what we normally do is deliberately 'routine' and 'practice' of language competences. To introduce problem-solving, we must first think about the ways languages are 'used' in Content-Based Instruction, if the teacher of the 'content' takes a problem-solving approach. We will return to this in more detail later, but if you now think back to the examples and scenarios in Chapter 1, you may notice that the focus often shifts from *practice* of the familiar, of 'the routine,' to *use* of language competences to solve problems as (intercultural) citizens. That is, the problems in the scenarios are mid-way between the opposing aims Beghetto (2018) describes, enabling students to develop complex problem-solving skills.

Furthermore, these problems engage students with *manageable* uncertainty; they are complex in that not all of the information required to find a solution or the approaches/strategies that lead to it are apparent at the outset, and may seem opaque at times. Yet since the contexts relate so closely to their lives, they have room to interact with the problem at different levels (cognitively/experientially) and in different ways (individually/collectively) that let them confront the uncertainty with a confidence that enables them to come up with their own choices for how they may want to tackle it. In this sense, the problem also enables the agentic engagement Beghetto (2018) explores.

To support the agentic engagement, you can ask your students four important questions in their reflection journals over the course of a project while assessing their understanding and supporting their development as problem-solvers at each stage. Beghetto (2017) developed these questions in the context of legacy challenges, but we consider them useful here. (When he mentions 'legacy projects,' he refers to complex problems as described above.)

1. *What is the problem?* As with many creative endeavors, legacy projects start with students identifying or finding a problem worth solving. Students are presented with the challenge of identifying an ill-defined or non-routine problem facing them, their school, community, or beyond.

2. *Why does it matter?* Once students have identified a problem, they must establish a rationale or argument for why the problem matters. This includes: clarifying whom the problem affects, what would happen if it is not addressed, and why addressing it is worth the effort.

3. *What are we going to do about it?* This question aims to invite students to take action and develop a plan for how they can productively resolve the uncertainty of the problem they identified.

4. *What lasting contribution will our project make?* This final question aims to help students consider how the work of the project will make a positive contribution beyond its life. This requires students to develop and implement a plan to sustain, maintain and curate the work of their project (p. 991).

While these questions were designed for application in a specific subject (e.g., math), Beghetto (2017) acknowledges that "in most cases they [students] will need a blend of knowledge and skills representing various academic domains to address the problems they are facing" (p. 992). This is one of the reasons why the interdisciplinary approach we propose in this book can be invaluable for our students' development of complex problem-solving skills.

Furthermore, the skills for complex problem-solving do not necessarily develop instinctively. We recommend you offer your students explicit support to develop these skills in a way transferable to other settings and contexts. For starters, choose language and activities that nurture a classroom culture of problem-solvers. This entails acknowledgment that it is normal to 'get stuck' in the problem-solving process, that a certain amount of struggle is to be expected and confronted. Explain to your students that challenges and failures are signs of growth from which they need to learn and plan to move forward (sometimes this requires moving a few steps back and correcting the course of action). You can help them see this by looking together at an example from the class or your own experience. Walk through the challenge with your students and unpack what happened, how they/you saw through it, and how the challenge helped them make progress toward the final goal.

One useful approach is to periodically check in with them about challenges they have faced and what they did about those challenges. From your findings you can create a class list of 'Strategies to Overcome Struggles' that they can refer to over time as needed, and that grows with you as the groups face new challenges. You can put the strategies on chart paper on the wall, or post on a shared website, or a handout that is revised with new strategies as they surface in the class.

Help your students reflect on the process by asking them, for example "What gave you trouble?" and then "How did you get unstuck?" or "What was your first step? What are you doing now? What might you try next?" You can ask these questions in the class, but we recommend you also have them write the answers as journal entries, which will be helpful to them but also to you for creating your list of strategies.

In facilitating complex problem-solving, you will not necessarily know all the answers, approaches, or paths. Students must know this, too, and understand that you are not there to solve the problems for them. You are there to coach them so they can solve problems for themselves. Create a classroom atmosphere where they can see that you are there to support them, brainstorm possible paths, point out resources, and so on. They can see you as a harness to rely on but must know that they are accountable for their own progress through finding a solution. This will help them become more independent and productive as they apply and adapt their thinking when engaging in future complex tasks.

We now turn to research in language teaching and learning to support the rationale and more tools for teaching languages for interdisciplinary Intercultural Citizenship.

3. How is teaching languages for interdisciplinary Intercultural Citizenship supported by current research in language teaching and learning?

In this section we contextualize the development of a rationale for interdisciplinary Intercultural Citizenship teaching in some current research in Second Language Acquisition and in language teaching and learning. We hope it will inspire you to engage in further reading to find your own individual reasons and explanations, especially since this is only one way to make the argument.

We saw that teaching languages without links to students' lives is one reason why progress in language learning is slow and competence unsatisfactory. Languages are often taught in a decontextualized way due to a common fear among language teachers that students do not learn the language unless teachers focus mostly on teaching its forms. However, we would like to draw your attention to what we see as pitfalls of approaches that focus too much on linguistic aspects.

For example, we might all remember the experience of language lessons in which we were asked or asked students ourselves, "What color is my sweater?" As Laura Terrill argued at the 2016 Connecticut Council of Language Teachers (CTCOLT) Fall Conference, that question makes sense only when the asker is color-blind. In other words, with such a question students are not challenged cognitively, other than recalling the correct word for the color. No new information is exchanged or learned. No critical thinking is involved. This information is irrelevant to students' lives except as practice of a formal aspect of the language.

Furthermore, language teachers and textbook writers have usually presented these formal aspects of language in a progression from "simple" to "complex." This notion of progression may be significant (although this, too, is arguable), but we are generally are not bound to a specific progression of content. We can help students investigate any topic in any order while they learn and use the language. One approach to this that has shown promise is content-based instruction (CBI), or content-and-language integrated learning (CLIL), as it is called in Europe. Already in 1997 in an overview on content-based instruction, Grabe & Stoller (1997) concluded:

> Content-based instruction is a powerful innovation in language teaching across a wide range of instructional contexts. There is strong empirical support for CBI, and the support of many well-documented programs offers additional support for the approach. Moreover, numerous practical features of CBI make it an appealing curricular approach to language instruction. (p. 19)

ACTFL subsequently endorsed CBI as a research priority (Glisan & Donato, 2012). More recently, Larsen-Freeman (2018, p. 65) identified CBI as "an obvious growth area" for the next years.

CBI and CLIL are usually associated with lessons other than language lessons. Other disciplines are taught in a TL, usually by the discipline specialists who have sufficient competence in the language to ensure learners acquire the knowledge and skills of, for example, science lessons. In the examples we developed in the previous chapters, it is the language teacher who is teaching content and drawing from another content area, cooperating in interdisciplinary teaching with teachers of other subjects— who continue to teach in the school's language—and in that sense the language teacher is doing CBI in the language classroom.

Previous chapters have also stressed choosing cognitively challenging topics relevant to students' lives and sometimes difficult and sensitive to discuss. This is because we do not want to infantilize our students, but to help them sharpen their critical understanding of the world. Ennser-Kananen (2016) wrote that, in language education, "We don't usually listen to stories of escaping war and finding refuge and racism in a new land, despite the fact that these events occur in settings where so many of the languages taught in classrooms around the world are spoken" (p. 557). This view is well supported by authors of work on critical pedagogy, with arguments and tools for teaching language for social justice, thereby helping students understand important matters of injustice and inequality (Nieto, 2009; Osborn, 2006; Reagan & Osborn, 2002; Glynn, Wesely & Wassell, 2014).

Projects in which language educators implemented Intercultural Citizenship showed that topics in which students investigate social justice issues and problems we face today lend themselves well to this way of teaching. For example, students can investigate issues in their community, such as immigration, and learn current misconceptions concerning immigration (Wallace & Tamborello-Noble, 2018) or discover issues of gender inequality through comparison of (a) gender roles in fairy tales and today (Meredith, Geyer & Wagner, 2018) or (b) the portrayal of gender regarding famous personalities (Wagner & Tracksdorf, 2018). Human rights can also become an important topic, as in a project conducted by Yulita & Porto (2017) dealing with human rights violations during the 1978 Soccer World Cup held during the Argentinian military dictatorship.

A similar development to Intercultural Citizenship education is the concept of 'intercultural service-learning,' a more recent development with the same combination of formal learning and service to the community, which is characteristic of established approaches but includes intercultural learning. The community in question may be culturally complex, for example, an immigrant community; Scenario D in Chapter 1 might be characterized as intercultural service-learning. It greatly overlaps with Intercultural Citizenship education, and the two can learn from each other (Rauschert & Byram, 2018).

Notable trends in other subjects relate their subject areas to issues of social justice. For example, the mathematical community has been concerned with people's apathy toward using mathematics to help them understand, and potentially change, important issues that adversely affect their lives, such as injustice, racial inequalities, and gentrification. To change this, we must address it at the school level; that is, present students with curricula that let them draw on their mathematical knowledge to solve problems important to their lives and society.

One program that has successfully done so is The Algebra Project, developed in the 1980s by high school teacher Robert Moses, whose work started with one school and expanded to over 200 over a decade. The project is nationally recognized for its focus on fostering social change regarding exclusion and regression of minorities by helping them understand their responsibility in gaining access to powerful mathematical ideas and equipping them with the tools to solve problems relevant to their lives (Moses & Cobb, 2001). Educators and researchers agree that, without attention to students' cultural backgrounds, mathematics classrooms will continue to produce and maintain many of society's inequities (Gutstein, 2003; Oakes, Joseph, & Muir, 2004).

Teaching for social justice is a notable movement toward teaching mathematics with social justice and cultural relevance in mind. Social justice pedagogy builds on the foundations for critical pedagogy expounded by Paulo Freire (1993) and on Marilyn Frankenstein's critical mathematical literacy (1990). Mathematics teaching for social justice helps students learn to use mathematics as a critical tool to understand social life, one's position in society, and issues of power and oppression, and to transform society into a more just system (Gonzalez, 2009).

In a social justice approach to mathematical education, students, for example, may create mathematically-based arguments to support conclusions addressing concerns about racism and classism in their community (Gutstein, 2006; Tate, 1995; Turner & Strawhun, 2005). To do so, they examine housing patterns in their relevant neighborhoods. For instance, they gather information corresponding to factors they consider relevant to the problem, such as census data, historical pricing data, wages and living expenses, and surveys of homeowners, homebuyers, and realtors. Then they analyze these by race and social class according to census data, calculate price averages considering houses' costs and sizes and wage differences, plot curves that let them determine pricing appreciation and depreciation, compare these graphs to determine interrelationships between race and class, compare responses to their surveys, and interpret the results of such comparisons.

Classrooms like these involve students with mathematics at a level at which they can form their own evaluation and critique of society's structures and underlying ideologies, which in turn support their development of individual and social agency (Gutstein, 2006). The motivation for teaching mathematics for social justice is informed citizenship (Moses & Cobb, 2001) and self-empowerment (Leonard, 2009; Martin, 2009; Sleeter, 1997), an issue of concern abroad as well as in the U.S., as evidenced in the most recent *Handbook of International Research in Mathematics Education*. For example, in the Priorities section about Strategies for Powerful Mathematics, Malloy (2010) writes:

> As students become more aware of social justice, we must present them with problems that not only tackle issues affecting their communities, but also reveal the motivations and the hidden agenda in their world... When students use and apply mathematical knowledge in such situations, they are learning to think critically about world issues and their environment... Through this process students will have an understanding of the inequities in society and will be able to critique the mathematical foundations of social situations—a skill that they will take through their lives (p. 42).

The unprecedented effects of social, cultural, and political factors on education is now internationally acknowledged in mathematics education, in research and practice (Morgan, 2014; Phakeng, Halai, Valero, Wagner, & Walshaw, 2014). The work to continue to develop curricula that support teaching mathematics for social justice is ongoing, yet more needs to be done.

We now turn to the next question.

4. How can this approach help educators in their advocacy for all language learners and for languages for all?

Let's begin with a few questions to ponder.

Pause TO Ponder

1. From what you have read about teaching languages for interdisciplinary Intercultural Citizenship, what are some arguments that will help you advocate among colleagues and others for language learners using this approach? What are some practical considerations? What do students learn? How can this approach contribute to society overall?

2. What are some opportunities language teachers have because of the knowledge and skills they have? (Some areas to consider are knowledge of how languages are learned; awareness of the connections between language(s), culture(s), and identities; knowledge about the necessity of language proficiency to acquire content knowledge in the TL and of strategies to facilitate learning content in another language.)

3. Do you think language teachers have certain obligations regarding their advocacy for all language learners, not only those in their own classrooms?

As we stated in Chapter 3, "If we do our job right, we can help our students communicate with those who speak a different language, hold a different opinion or come from a different cultural background, but also help them become mediators for people who otherwise could not communicate with each other" (p. 37). We have also argued, in answering the first question in this chapter, that language learners benefit from language education in a more 'esoteric' way: they can lead a richer life because they understand themselves and the world better. This also has implications for social justice issues. Because we reflect on the connections between language(s), culture(s), and identities as part of our training and daily jobs, we are aware of the effects misconceptions about heritage languages and emergent bilingualism can have on society.

We have learned and are interested in how we learn languages, how being discouraged from using one's L1 can hamper us from learning other content in school and developing a healthy identity regarding one's heritage. We have learned (or can investigate) how content can be taught to emergent bilinguals using strategies that let them use their L1 and their L2 to access the learning material. Rivers & Brecht, (2018, p. 30) emphasize, "Expanded capacity in "America's languages" is also a social imperative, and the provision of language access in the delivery of social services is mandated under Title VI of the Civil Rights Act of 1964 and the Affordable Care Act. This mandate underscores the need for expanded language-enabled services as a growing number of American citizens speak languages other than English..."

1. Have you found yourself with an opportunity to address a myth about emergent bilingualism or multilingualism? For example, one myth we often hear is that emergent bilinguals do not learn English (in an English-speaking environment) if they use their L1 (which is a language other than English). Of course, plenty of research refutes this claim, but some research proves just the opposite. Can you think of other myths?
2. What are some practical activities you can think of that we can engage in to advocate for all language learners?
3. Can you imagine providing resources for your colleagues who would like to know more about teaching strategies for teaching emergent bilinguals?
4. What implications does the quote above by Rivers & Brecht (2018) have for language educators?

One implication you may have thought about from the Rivers & Brecht (2018) quote is that we, as world languages teachers, must also draw on our resources in heritage language speakers. This is supported by Abbott et al. (2014), who say that their vision "includes heritage language learners and English Language Learners (ELL) as well as native English speakers acquiring abilities in a world language" (p. 6). This in turn necessitates a change in perspective from a deficit view of emergent bilinguals who lack something to appreciating them as resources, as people who, like us, already speak their L1 and now happen to learn another one. Although this view should be nothing new to language educators, widespread misconceptions about emergent bilinguals in schools as well as in communities still prevail. This leads to numerous problems that arise in some but not all situations:

> **Widespread misconceptions about emergent bilinguals in schools as well as in communities still prevail.**

- Students are discouraged from or even forbidden to, use their L1 in class or in public places in the school.

- Students are discouraged from taking a third language as a subject, because it is feared they will be overloaded with schoolwork.

- Students cannot develop their plurilingual identities, because of the implicit messages about their home languages and cultures they are exposed to every day.

1. If you look at your school and other schools you know, what is the general view of emergent bilinguals (students who come to your country with an L1 other than that of your environment)?
2. What is available for these students in terms of language education?
3. Are the students "allowed" to use their L1 in the classrooms, the hallways and the schools? Why do you think this language-use policy is in place?
4. Are students allowed or encouraged to take another language, or are they rather discouraged from doing so?

So far we have promoted the idea that you can advocate for all language learners, in the sense that we can help avoid misconceptions about language learners and language learning, especially those created by differentiating emergent bilinguals from other language learners. At the beginning of the chapter we also introduced the mission statement by the Commission on Language Learning (American Academy of Arts and Sciences, 2017) that language education should be available to all students. This, as we mentioned above, entails advocacy for language education for all, and for understanding and working on expanding the resource available to us.

We, as language educators, can become thoughtful advocates for all language learners and for languages for all. We can empower our students by developing their understanding of important and complex issues, including those related to identities, and we can advocate for all language learners in our interactions with our colleagues and with all stakeholders who might have misconceptions that we can address by sharing our expertise. A big step in this direction would be to prepare language educators—those teaching English to emergent bilinguals, as well as those teaching languages other than English—together (Tedick & Walker, 1994; Osborn, 2006) so they could learn together and exchange information about the bigger picture of language education, such as the role of language in our students' identities. This way of thinking about language teaching might require us to examine our identities as language teachers, i.e., what we see as our responsibilities and tasks. This leads to our last question in this chapter.

5. How does this approach relate to our professional identities?

May we first ask you to reflect on your own professional identity/identities? We use the plural as well, because we often wear "multiple hats" in our professional lives.

Issues related to identity can be tricky. We do not want to tell you who you should be as a language educator. However, we will share our vision. Throughout this book we have supported a conceptualization of language education as a mission central to the education of all students and the development of their identities. This means helping them investigate important concepts and opening their and our minds to injustices that happen due to misconceptions about languages and cultures. Facilitating our

1. How would you describe yourself regarding your professional identity? Are you primarily a language teacher? Are you a language and culture teacher, or even a 'languaculture' teacher?
2. To teach interdisciplinary Intercultural Citizenship, do you feel you need to change your perspectives of (a) language education, (b) your role in the classroom, (c) your students' roles, (d) your colleagues' roles, etc.?

students' Intercultural Citizenship also means enabling them to critically investigate their world and make sound judgments based on specific evidence and diverse perspectives, and providing them with the resources to advocate for themselves and their needs in (language) education.

Therefore, we see ourselves as not only teachers of language and related cultures but also educators for interdisciplinary Intercultural Citizenship. This way of teaching entails looking beyond the borders of our curricula and classrooms, and also beyond national borders. In other words, we help our students to solve complex issues in the here and now and to continue to learn and gain experiences for future problem-solving and collaboration. This requires us to encourage our students to pool all the resources available. Rather than thinking exclusively about the language curriculum, we help them do something with the language. What they do can depend on their interests and/or essential social issues. In prior chapters we gave examples of what can happen when we do that. Embracing a borderless classroom is a wonderful experience.

However, we must jettison the illusion that the teacher has to be the "knower." Instead, we become fellow investigators with our students. We provide strategies to evaluate information and draw from a variety of resources, which involves practicing and teaching Intellectual Humility. This requires our students and us to investigate multiple perspectives of complex topics that can be discomforting or sound offensive, especially when our own or our students' convictions are challenged, particularly in a language in which we lack high proficiency. While this might cause some educators to shy away from such topics, we feel the opposite urge: to prepare our students exactly for such situations in real life. We do not want them to fear discussing diverging opinions; instead, we want to give them the tools to work through difference,

To shed light on this issue, we now share some experiences and lessons we learned from an interdisciplinary project we engaged in a few years ago. It teamed our university's Departments of Mathematics, Education, and Literatures, Cultures and Languages with the departments of Social Studies, Science, Mathematics and World Languages in a public middle school in Connecticut. Manuela and Fabiana co-taught two seminars for graduate students in those three university departments with the goal of developing our graduate students' understanding of how to meaningfully integrate Intercultural Citizenship into education. Mike was also on the team, and colleagues from the school and the three of us communicated regularly with each other and with the students. The final product comprised unit plans shared with our colleagues in the middle school.

One lesson we learned from this is that we must respect disciplinary understandings and boundaries. That is, we must be aware of our own disciplinary understanding, bias, definitions, practices, confusion and uncertainty concerning specific focal questions, problems and topics, and we should help our colleagues develop these understandings. For example, when we worked with graduate students from Mathematics and Literatures, Cultures and Languages, we first made sure Fabiana met with her Mathematics students and Manuela met with her Literatures, Cultures, and Languages students, so that both groups could view their own expectations, understandings and hesitations before we met in a whole group. This strategy assured our students that they did not need to lose their own professional identity to be part of this interdisciplinary project and the process of co-designing interdisciplinary Intercultural Citizenship units for a middle school.

We also learned the importance of genuine interdisciplinary work. Rather than simply adding one discipline to the other, we truly integrated them to make something greater than the sum of the disciplines. To do so, we constantly pushed ourselves to help our students and ourselves combine our understandings and expand them beyond our disciplines.

We also learned the importance of a collaborative environment in which it was okay to not know and to ask without losing face. Manuela, Fabiana and Mike modelled this behavior by asking questions and admitting to not knowing something. We also developed sessions in which we figured out who brought which expertise to the table and how we could all benefit from each other's experiences and knowledge. Finally, from experiences in other projects, we anticipated moments of frustration, so we turned teachable moments into true learning opportunities. In other projects we learned that such bumps in the road can teach us important lessons, and we welcomed new ones in this bigger interdisciplinary project.

So what does this mean? Language educators tend to be seen, and perhaps see themselves, as 'a French teacher,' 'a German teacher,' or perhaps 'a French and German teacher,' but the reference is always to language and the task of teaching and learning a difficult 'subject.' Important as this may be, it no longer suffices, and we must rethinking our professional identities, as a matter of not only personal satisfaction with executing a worthwhile task but also public recognition of the social and political significance of language teaching in its new guise.

Here we promote a more complex, enriched understanding of language teaching that helps students reflect critically on their own identities as well as the dynamic processes of communication in which they engage in diverse contexts. This understanding ensures that language or languaculture teaching is related directly to the learners' world. Rather than learning discrete aspects of language to 'apply' later, in this approach we encourage students to immediately apply what they learn to analyze the world around them and make critical judgments based on specific evidence. We provide tools for students to learn important information in another language by interacting with others, often in real time, in the TL. Thus students see language education and the important knowledge, attitudes and skills they acquire as something they use right now and will continue to use.

Our vision requires change. Language educators must critically examine their own professional identities and their views of language and culture as well as language education and its goals. This likely entails stepping out of one's comfort zone by, for example, exploring unfamiliar content with students or collaborating with somebody in a different subject area. This process might require skills similar to those found in Intercultural Competence. Ultimately, this can lead to a reconceptualization of language education as a crucial contributor to a number of educational missions. By teaching languages through a more holistic approach, and through content relevant to the students' lives and society, we foster critical thinking skills while teaching relevant knowledge about the world. Furthermore, through collaborative projects with other subjects, we help students understand the utility of language education in their lives beyond classroom walls.

Conclusion

In Chapter 5, we contextualized and considered the bigger picture for ourselves and you as language teachers. We hope this has given you arguments and evidence you might need in discussions with other teachers, administrators, students, parents, and other stakeholders.

In the next chapter, we turn to practical questions and ways of moving forward.

Moving forward
—PRACTICAL CONSIDERATIONS

In this chapter, we close the circle with a set of FAQs teachers brought up while embarking on or considering this work. To make this journey successful and efficient, we offer practical suggestions for the question raised in Chapter 5 of how language teachers can collaborate with each other and with teachers from other disciplines to become advocates for all language learners. Finally, we discuss how we can move forward with teaching languages for Intercultural Citizenship using an interdisciplinary approach.

Introduction

Teachers receive numerous tasks and challenges daily, and it is understandable when they say they don't need more work. Teaching in the ways described in earlier chapters would no doubt require you to rethink the way you see your task as a language teacher. You would ask yourself how you might become a languaculture teacher cooperating with teachers of other subjects/disciplines to help students become active citizens in their local and global communities. This is no simple matter.

Yet we have found in our work with teachers that what we recommend speaks to their interests as educators concerned with their students as people, not just as language learners. This is clear in the stories that they have told and we helped them to publish (Byram et al., 2017; Wagner et al., 2018). Nonetheless, we and they have also met with difficulties, which we described in the same books. We must acknowledge the difficulties rather than pretend they don't exist. More importantly, we learned that challenges helped us grow and learn, and presented opportunities to improve on what we did and develop important competences in our students and ourselves.

In this book we have also tried to address the potential difficulties that have probably been going through your mind as you read. We hope each chapter's 'Pause to Ponder' sections have helped, and, in this final chapter, we have collected some FAQs from our experience in using the ideas, with assistance from our collaborators. Some questions below were asked when we elicited comments on Facebook and Twitter. Sometimes teachers allowed us to use their names; other times they preferred to remain anonymous.

The crucial point is that success comes from teachers working together. This happens easily enough among teachers of the same discipline, when language teachers collaborate to innovate. When working with people of other disciplines, it can be harder to build understanding and trust, but we have found in our practice that it works and is an enriching experience for everyone involved if you are open-minded and willing to solve problems as they occur. So here are some questions teachers have asked us, followed by our honest answers, which are not always solutions. Often solutions are yet to be found or must be sought in the specific contexts in which you work.

Frequently Asked Questions
Questions about teachers

Beckie asks: *How do I teach ICC when I don't know the ins and outs of all target cultures? I know the answer has to do with teaching kids to notice and not teaching stereotypes, but I am thinking of people who don't have access to native speakers or travel.*

Beckie's question is very frequent and completely understandable. Teachers are usually expected to be 'knowers.' However, the main focus in teaching Intercultural Competence is not the transmission of information about a foreign country, though students may expect that. The purpose is to help them understand how they themselves can find out more about the people with whom they are communicating wherever they come from—including from within their own country, how intercultural interaction takes place, and how their perceptions of other people and other people's perceptions of them influence the success of communication. This latter point is what Beckie refers to when she mentions 'not teaching stereotypes.' Furthermore, although the focus will be on people who speak the language students are learning, the skills and attitudes they learn in the language classroom are transferable to other kinds of interaction and communication. This is an advantage of teaching skills and attitudes rather than facts about a country.

Additional Reading

Stereotypes and Prejudice

- Abrams, D. (2010) *Processes of Prejudice: Theory, evidence and intervention.* Manches▮ UK: Equality and Human Rights Commissior▮

- Hughes, C. (2017) *Understanding Prejudice and Education.* London: Routledge.

And the still important classic work:

- Allport, G. 1954, *The Nature of Prejudice.* Cambridge, Mass.: Addison-Wesley.

So a teacher need not know everything about 'the target culture'—a phrase best avoided, since it is used as a synonym for 'country,' and it is better to say 'country' when we mean it. It is in any case impossible for the teacher to know everything, and in fact many cultures may be associated with a particular language, for example, many nations where Spanish is spoken as the L1, and within those countries are many variations on beliefs, values and behaviors people share. A country may also have numerous regional dialects (e.g., China) or different languages (e.g., India) that are so different that speakers cannot understand each other, in addition to differences in beliefs and customs; in other words, many cultures. Furthermore, being a native speaker of the language being taught and learned has no particular advantage. The non-native speaker has all of the skills and knowledge needed to teach intercultural communicative competence.

Of course, learners need some factual information about other countries where the TL is spoken, but this is available to teachers (and learners) in reference books, on the Internet, etc. This kind of information does not depend on having been to the countries in question, and when one does visit another country, one does not acquire this kind of information.

Regarding the latter part of Beckie's question, you do not need access to a native speaker. You and your students can also invite (virtually or in person) colleagues, friends, members of the local community, etc., who have experiences with certain topics and might even have lived in an area you are exploring through the classroom project and activities. Such interactions give students and you an additional point of view they can consider in their investigations. This is also where cross-curricular dimensions and interdisciplinarity come into focus to highlight the point that intercultural education need not be linked to languages and culture(s) alone, but can extend to the exchange of information and experience on content subjects across the curriculum.

Melina asks: *How do I answer questions from colleagues such as "I don't teach language, I teach math, art, history, geography, biology. Why should intercultural communicative competence be my business?" Or:"I don't teach civics, I teach math, language, art, history, geography, biology. Why should Intercultural Citizenship be my business?"*

These two questions are what language educators seeking interdisciplinary collaboration may hear from colleagues. Our view, which is not unique to us by any means, is that the curricula of schools have become too focused on subjects and not enough on learners. Grammatically the verb 'to teach' has two objects: "I teach people (not 'students') mathematics, geography, etc." For some this might appear to be a grammatical nuance (i.e., a verb with two objects), but teachers in all subjects often forget the first object, and forget that they are people, not just students. In light of this, we have presented in this book calls for content and dispositions teachers in many different subjects are asked to address in their teaching that are undeniably linked with Intercultural Citizenship and with each other. In addition, given the constraints standardized tests place on teachers of subjects such as math, your colleagues in these areas will welcome new ways to offer students opportunities to revisit, use, and explain content knowledge in other contexts that link back to the original subject area's expectations. ACTFL provides excellent resources showing the connections and interconnectedness of the *Common Core Standards* and the *World-Readiness Standards for Learning Languages* with other subjects.

In addition, these questions must be answered not in terms of subjects but to ensure that students experience the whole curriculum as coherent and see relationships among subjects, how they complement each other. This is, of course, not easy. Particularly teachers in secondary education and faculty in postsecondary institutions, including language educators, tend to think of themselves primarily as teachers of subjects, whereas teachers in elementary schools tend to be less subject-oriented. Once you have re-oriented your own way of thinking, it requires care not to 'preach' to others. Others may be persuaded more by good examples than by 'philosophy', and we hope the scenarios in Chapter 1 might help you in your discussions with other teachers.

> **❝ As one tries these ideas, it becomes easier to plan, and teaching for Intercultural Citizenship becomes second nature. ❞**

Melina asks: How are teachers expected to develop interdisciplinary projects? In their own time? In practical terms, how should collaboration take place? Should schools provide the necessary conditions related to time, resources, or collaborative structures?

Melina implicitly answers this question herself: 'In an ideal world schools should indeed provide the time, resources, and structures, and we hope this will be the case for you.' Yet we know that practice may be different and the extra work will be in your own time. That is why we have provided detailed examples we hope you can adapt to your own circumstances. Once you have shown what is possible and the value of this kind of teaching, school administrators will more likely see the potential and make special arrangements. This is about creating a mindset so that each next activity related to the shift—be it planning daily lessons, designing more effective units of instruction, creating common summative assessments of language performance, or a long-range curriculum redesign—will be that much easier and less time-consuming. With practice, this will simply become the way to do our work, and collaborating across disciplinary boundaries will be commonplace.

Another possibility is for collaborators to apply for funding through grants that could be available through school districts, educational organizations, research foundations, local, state or national governments, and even private industry. Depending on your district or university policies, such grants can buy you some time in the form of partial teaching releases or reimburse you for materials or indeed the extra time you spend on the projects.

But more importantly, we feel that this way of teaching can become a mindset, and with mutual support of colleagues and with some practice it need not take additional time to teach this way. As one tries these ideas, it becomes easier to plan, and teaching for Intercultural Citizenship becomes second nature. The question of how a topic relates to the students' lives becomes easier to answer, as students are also more tuned into the necessary processes, hence more actively involved in the planning. Additionally, the connections we make tend to continue, so collaboration becomes less work-intensive and more natural.

Questions about language proficiency

Melina asks: *Can intercultural communicative competence and Intercultural Citizenship be developed with students with low language proficiency (whether in native or foreign/second languages)?*

There are certainly limits to what can be done entirely in a second language when students' proficiency is still low. Yet we know from experience—as described in the books and articles we have published (Wagner, Conlon Perugini, & Byram, 2018; Meredith, Geyer, & Wagner, 2018)—that more is possible than at first seems likely. Teachers can use a number of techniques to help students think deeply and critically in the TL. For example, as soon as students know numbers, tables and figures are accessible and become helpful ways to present complex information. Pictures provide a wealth of resources. If your classroom has a strict TL-only approach, students can use their L1 to reflect more deeply on issues for homework outside of class. In Chapters 3 and 4 we offered some example prompts for these types of reflections, particular to those units but easily adaptable to your own context. The NCSSFL-ACTFL Intercultural Reflection Tool can also be a source of prompts and questions for different proficiency levels. Once the language limits are reached, cooperation in an interdisciplinary project means issues can be taken up by other teachers.

Another approach is to allow 'translanguaging,' i.e., students using a combination of languages to express their ideas. This may sound like mixing languages and is anathema to some teachers, but it is normal practice among people who are naturally bilingual, e.g., have spoken two or more languages from birth or early childhood. Through translanguaging, students can use all of their linguistic resources to learn content and develop their additional languages. This approach also highlights viewing emergent bilinguals' linguistic and cultural backgrounds as resources rather than as a deficit. We recommend that you decide which strategies can help you and your students achieve the objectives and also allow them to express themselves fully while acquiring the TL.

Additional Reading

Translanguaging, Language Architecture, and Language Exploration

- Wei, Li (2018). Translanguaging as a Practical Theory of Language. *Applied Linguistics 39*, 1: 9–30.

This is an open access article.

- Flores, N. (2016). Combatting Marginalized Spaces in Education through Language Architecture. *Perspectives in Urban Education* 13, 1-3.

- García, O., & Wei, L. (2014). *Translanguaging: Language, Bilingualism and Education.* Palgrave Macmillan.

Melina asks: *Does interdisciplinary teaching require a certain minimum level of language proficiency in students, in particular in foreign/second language contexts, to be feasible?*

The answer to Melina's question is in one sense simple. Teachers must attend to cognitive development in interdisciplinary teaching the way they do in their usual approach to planning their teaching. There are, however, some interesting further features of interdisciplinary work. For language teachers, the value of inter-disciplinary teaching is that they see what cognitively demanding work their students do in other subjects, which they cannot as easily do in a foreign language. Similarly, different teachers see that different subjects make different kinds of demands; this, too, provides refreshing insights. When teachers work as an interdisciplinary team, their professional knowledge and intuitions lead to creative teaching, as we saw from the scenarios of Chapter 1 and the discussion of planning in later chapters.

Additional Reading

Intercultural Dimension of Language Teaching

- Byram, M., Gribkova, B., & Starkey, H. (2002) *Developing the intercultural dimension in language teaching: A practical introduction for teachers.*

This resource has 12 key questions, each answered in a couple of pages, with further suggestions for practical approaches. You can download it free from: https://www.coe.int/en/web/platform-plurilingual-intercultural-language-education/foreign-languages# {%2228070229%22:[2], %2228070247%22:[

Questions about students

Mei asks: *What to do to develop Intercultural Competence in students at different levels, ages, ethnic and social backgrounds? Are there striking differences?*

The question of different ages must be addressed, as with all teaching. (We discuss this below in answer to another question.) Regarding different ethnic and social backgrounds or contexts, every context requires different approaches and a different kind of preparation on the teacher's part. For example, some groups we teach might have ample opportunity to interact with differences because of the composition of different backgrounds within the group itself. In other situations, teachers might face a seemingly homogenous group. In both contexts, they must help students interact with different perspectives and values, as well as different practices and products. Ideally, students have enough opportunity to reflect on issues from various perspectives to create a change in their own perspective(s). How these goals will be achieved will vary. While it would be ideal to have access to members of different cultural groups, this is not always possible. In such cases (remote areas without ready access to the Internet), scenarios or videos could be creatively used.

Additional Reading

A key book, mentioned already in Chapter 2, to help you understand the perceptions, prejudice and stereotypes that young people have is:

- Barrett, M. (2007) *Children's knowledge, beli and feelings about nations and national groups.* New York: Psychology Press – Taylor and Francis Group.

For additional information on Intercultural Com municative Competence in educational exchang you will find the following book valuable:

- Fantini, A. (2018). *Intercultural communi- cative competence in educational exchange A multinational perspective.* New York: Routledge.

A further question often asked is: *You are asking me as a teacher to encourage my students to become politically active, but how can I justify this to parents and principals?*

This is a fundamental question with different dimensions:

1. First of all, we need to be clear about what is meant by 'political.' We see all activity in public life and—in the examples we have given—in local communities as 'political.' This is not a matter of party or partisan politics; it is just what we all do as active members of a society trying to improve things for everyone. However, we know that the word 'political' often creates the wrong connotations when people hear about our work, so it is necessary to say what we mean.

   Mike begins his lectures with dictionary definitions of 'political' and 'politics':
   Oxford English Dictionary: Political = Relating to or concerned with public life and affairs as involving questions of authority and government; relating to or concerned with the theory or practice of politics. AND Politics = The political ideas, beliefs, or commitments of a particular individual, organization, etc.

   He then offers this definition:
   Learners being or becoming political **= develop** their own ideas, beliefs and commitments—become **involved** in public life—**'practice politics'**—challenge authority [at any level – family, school, sports club, national and international government].

   The key ideas are highlighted in bold, and we think that most if not all teachers would agree that 'developing ideas,' becoming 'involved' in practical politics/ activities, are necessary purposes in education. Most, too, would agree that we want our learners to 'challenge', and be independent thinkers. Being 'political' in this sense is therefore not problematic as an aim for teaching.

   Colleagues who have been promoting teaching for social justice have run into similar issues, in line with their claim that, regardless of whether we are aware of it or not, as teachers we are political. Manuela creates activities in which she asks students to research the possible implications of what they teach, for example, based on material they teach from, including textbooks (Osborn, 2006). Questions teachers can ask themselves include, "Do I unwittingly promote a bias by not questioning what is presented in any material I teach?"

   The reality is similar for other subjects as well. For example, as we have presented in previous chapters, mathematics teachers are called to engage students with the subject in meaningful ways, to make the content relevant to students' lives, and to have students apply their knowledge in authentic situations. All of these are undeniably related to students becoming political (as described above) and to teachers reflecting on the role a well-selected activity or task can have in helping students develop the critical thinking skills they can later use to discern and evaluate information and decisions that will guide their participation in society.

2. The next point follows from this because, if being political means being an active citizen, then it is not controversial, since in many education systems, including in the U.S., this is considered to be a normal and important part of educational purposes. For example in the National Standards for Civics and Government, there is the following statement:

> The goal of education in civics and government is informed, responsible participation in political life by competent citizens committed to the fundamental values and principles of American constitutional democracy. Their effective and responsible participation requires the acquisition of a body of knowledge and of intellectual and participatory skills. [...] The family, religious institutions, the media, and community groups exert important influences. Schools, however, bear a special and historic responsibility for the development of civic competence and civic responsibility. Schools fulfill that responsibility through both formal and informal curricula beginning in the earliest grades and continuing through the entire educational process. (http://www.civiced.org/standards?page=stds_toc_intro)

If asked to justify what is done in the language classroom and in an interdisciplinary project, then we can refer to this argument and expect its acceptance. Again, we ask you to find your own position, but you know ours and that we feel obliged to help our students become critical thinkers and responsible world citizens. We consider this thinking beyond national borders as our task, because that is the nature of the subjects we teach and the topics we address.

3. A third dimension is the question of the age of students. Teachers in elementary and junior high school may wonder if they can or should urge their students to become active in their community, therefore 'political,' since they have a responsibility for them as (legally) 'children.' Teachers in high school and postsecondary education have a different role, as their students are (legally) adults or about to become so.

The responsibility of the first group of teachers is to teach the curriculum and educate young people as active citizens. Of course, they should make all aspects of their teaching age-appropriate, which applies to this aspect, too. However, in our experience teachers have found appropriate ways to involve their students in active work in their communities. Teachers in the second group are in a different position: they must leave adult students to make their own decisions and take responsibility for their own actions. This, too, has proved feasible and fruitful in our experience.

4. In preparing for 'political activity' in the sense we have described, learners and educators must often discuss the issues and problems in their community, as we saw in the Chapter 1 scenarios. Teachers have shared with us that they wonder if they should give their opinions about the problems; perhaps they fear accusation of wanting to influence even indoctrinate their students.

There are two basic approaches to this: (a) to take the role of the 'neutral chair,' which means the teacher encourages students to voice their opinions and the evidence they have for opinions, ensuring that everyone who wishes to speak is given a respectful hearing; and (b) to become involved, and students may ask their teachers for their views as people they respect. Here the teacher must, with proper intellectual humility, make their students aware that this is a personal view of an individual, not of someone using authority to impose.

Manuela had a wake-up moment when a student shared with her that in a language course at the university it can be difficult at times to voice what might be considered more conservative views. She therefore tries to make sure that students look at different perspectives, for example, by giving specific roles to students that they then must investigate. Students might have to explain or defend a view quite different from their own, which requires them to take a step back (suspend their judgment) and walk in somebody else's shoes. This is, of course, in line with developing Intercultural Competence and the larger Intercultural Citizenship.

Questions about integration with the *NCSSFL-ACTFL Can-Do Statements for Intercultural Communication*:

Beckie asks: *Many of us use a unit template where the Can-Do Statements align directly to the unit evaluation(s). How would you recommend integrating an Intercultural Communication Can-Do statement: as a separate goal or integrated?*

We will try to provide a simple 'solution' to this problem, and a more complex one. We could integrate what students 'can do' with the language and what they 'can do' in terms of our Intercultural Competence/Citizenship objectives. The overarching goal, for us, would always be an Intercultural Citizenship goal. For example: "I can participate in spontaneous spoken, written, or signed conversations on familiar topics, creating sentences and series of sentences to ask and answer a variety of questions in order to discover and evaluate important information concerning [add Intercultural Competence topic here]."

Another option is to use a more complex unit template (such as the one in Chapters 3 and 4) that lets you reflect in more detail on your goals for intercultural communication. You can also do both, as a more detailed reflection on the aspects we include in the unit template is crucial. In a sense we would say that we teach languages to teach Intercultural Citizenship, but you are best able to judge how you frame the intercultural component in your language teaching.

Questions about creating interdisciplinary approaches

Melina asks a number of questions about interdisciplinary teaching itself: *In which contexts/settings is interdisciplinary teaching sustainable? Are there particular settings in which it is not sustainable (e.g., in conflict-driven societies, with special needs students, specific populations like refugees, etc.)?*

The sustainability of interdisciplinary teaching depends on many factors. At a certain level, interdisciplinary teaching should be sustainable in almost any situation, as it mostly requires language teachers' openness to including concepts, strategies and skills from other disciplines and subjects. Larger-scale projects with multiple stakeholders involved require more effort and coordination. Then it will largely depend on participants' willingness to commit to the work and face challenges together. Participants in such projects should seek support in any way they can. Finally, we found it helpful for us to start small and branch out once we could see small successes.

The feasibility of teaching interdisciplinary Intercultural Citizenship units to different groups will depend on each case. In general, emergent bilinguals (students with an L1 other than the language of instruction) would gain much from this instruction, as their skills would benefit them and their classmates. Since this kind of teaching in our experience goes hand-in-hand with differentiated teaching and valuing the contribution and strengths of all students, it should also be an appropriate way to teach special education populations.

The answer to the last part of the question concerning the use of this way of teaching in conflict-driven societies or with refugees is multi-faceted. On the one hand, such populations need the tools to mediate peacefully and effectively even more. We aim to provide the tools to communicate with those who have different values, backgrounds, and opinions and to try to understand various positions better. (The example about working with refugees in Germany in Scenario D in Chapter 1 provides a starting point for thinking about similar situations elsewhere.) On the other hand, we can see potential problems if disenfranchised populations become penalized for activist behaviors. Teachers must therefore know the context well and advocate for those skills that help their students understand what is useful for them, e.g., situation analysis skills. Understanding what activities, if any, could be helpful in addressing injustices will be another important aspect in such environments.

Additional Reading

Interdisciplinary Teaching

We recommend the following papers and books about possibilities and challenges of interdisciplinary teaching:

- Beane, J. A. (1995). Curriculum integration and the disciplines of knowledge. *The Phi Delta Kappa, 76*(8), 616-622.

- Beane, J. A. (2016). *Curriculum integration: Designing the core of democratic education.* New York, NY: Teachers College Press.

- Drake, S. M., & Burns, R. C. (2004). *Meeting standards through integrated curriculum.* Alexandria, VA: ASCD.

Melina asks: *Is there a western bias in the rationale and foundations of interdisciplinary teaching?*

Caroline asks a related question: *What about countries where there is no democracy?*

Even research in intercultural or multicultural communication and education is inherently biased, as theoretical and empirical studies are often based on Western philosophy or data collected in white middle class populations. In the case of teaching students to engage in Intercultural Citizenship, we indeed presuppose a democratic society in which such behaviors, at least in theory, should not be punished, and we must follow our convictions that democracy in its best forms is important.

Another frequent question is: *In the context of an already overloaded curriculum, is interdisciplinary teaching not an extra unnecessary burden for teachers?*

The answer to this, in the long run, is to rethink the curriculum, but in the short term, teachers might think in terms of 'projects,' i.e., relatively short periods when the focus is on this way of teaching and leads to the kinds of outcome described in Chapter 1. Short projects of this kind can have massively disproportionate effects—a massive return for a small investment.

Dorie asks: *What do you do when parents are not on board? What if administrators or other teachers are not on board? Or if the teachers on your team are lacking in their own IC?*

Even in situations where interdisciplinary teaching (or for that matter, Intercultural Competence, global citizenship, etc.) seems to be an important part of the educational mission "on paper," "real support" often lacks or lags behind. If there is "support on paper but not in actions," we suggest that you often refer to the connections between your teaching outcomes and your school's or university's mission statement. If interdisciplinary teaching or teaching for Intercultural Citizenship is not explicitly valued, we suggest that you connect the outcomes to the educational mission in any way you can. In most contexts, we know such mission statements refer to students being able to solve problems and do something with their education.

Furthermore, we can seek commonalities and ask how we can support each other without necessarily calling what we do "interdisciplinary teaching."

In other words, as teachers, we often have to deal with realities that are not an ideal fit for our goals and objectives, but we almost always find ways to still do what we are convinced is important. For example, we have been told that connecting world language education with "teaching for social justice" was considered off-putting in a school district at a certain time. Would we then no longer teach our students to be critical thinkers and active citizens? The answer for us was to continue to do what we think is important without using terminology that caused friction at that specific time.

An important piece of advice we would like to give is to seek support from the community that is like-minded, from educational organizations such as ACTFL or local world language education organizations for world languages and NCTM or local mathematics education organizations. We also found support at our Humanities Institute and through grants. We belong to professional communities and share what we do but also ask for help there. We have had wonderful experiences when we reached out to such communities.

Additional Reading

Further Reading on how to teach languages for social justice includes:

- Osborn, T. A. (2006). *Teaching world languages for social justice: A sourcebook of principles and practices.* New York: Routledge.
- Glynn, C., Wesely, P., & Wassell, B. (2014). *Words and Actions: Teaching Languages through the Lens of Social Justice.* Alexandria, VA: American Council on the Teaching of Foreign Languages.

Melina asks: *Are there ethical considerations to keep in mind in interdisciplinary teaching?*

As in all teaching, there are bound to be ethical considerations when we engage in interdisciplinary teaching. We must clarify to students that we are not experts of another discipline but that we investigate with them and their teachings in the other disciplines ways we can apply what we learn to solve problems. This requires and develops intellectual humility on everybody's part, which we think is an important virtue to have. We also ensure that students are not penalized in other contexts because of the way we teach. As we mentioned, we need to be aware of possible negative consequences if this way of teaching is misunderstood in specific circumstances and be open with our students about it.

Finally, no matter how neutral we try to be in our teaching, we must be aware that we have biases and convictions in ourselves and we may occasionally influence our students in ways we do not intend. Our students might also find themselves in situations in which they have to face conflict due to what they learned. In an extreme interpretation of what we do, we would say it is still better that students have the tools to address issues and to face conflict.

The way forward

We now invite you to break through classroom walls and borders of all kinds—disciplinary, educational and national—to enjoy the numerous benefits of collaborating to teach languages for Intercultural Citizenship. This approach enables language educators to situate themselves front and center in the educational task of empowering students to participate actively in shaping their own future by starting to solve problems in the here and now. It also solves the conundrum of how to make education relevant for students. Since students apply what they learn immediately to problems of their interest, they will not be left with the question of how what they learned can possibly help them in the future. We have shared our approaches to language teaching that can be used to achieve the goals of Intercultural Citizenship. We do not believe they are the only ones, and we hope you will find other ways that will lead to good results. Whatever the approach, however, students must develop the knowledge, skills and attitudes related to Intercultural Communicative Competence as well as their language proficiency.

If students are asked to apply what they learn to real and often complex problems, interdisciplinary approaches are a *sine qua non*. The level of interdisciplinarity can be determined on a case-by-case basis. You may decide to start with a well-defined smaller problem to which students bring their knowledge and skills from other subject areas into your classroom and subject, or you might actively and officially collaborate with colleagues from different subjects in a project that runs throughout a school year. In either case—and in any version of interdisciplinary teaching in-between these ends of a continuum—we must be open to difference and to practice our own tolerance of ambiguity. In our experience, if we approach collaborations with such openness and intellectual humility, we will create situations in which all parties can learn from and with each other while acknowledging disciplinary boundaries and the contributions of everyone involved. We thus enable our students to begin to see connections among subjects and the ways in which they can use their newly gained understanding to contribute to their own community and others in and beyond their country's borders.

In this way, the language classroom is a means of bringing the work in other classrooms into a coherent whole with immediate implications and applications for students' communities in ways informed and enriched by the 'other.' For this is the strength of language teaching. By giving particular force to decentering and discovering how issues are addressed in other languages and cultures, students can begin to question what they otherwise assume is 'normal.'

In the same vein, as language educators we can help colleagues, parents and community members question myths related to language education. In the previous chapters we mentioned, for example, how emergent bilinguals are often viewed from a deficit perspective. With the approach presented here we can show students their opportunities, thereby facilitating a healthy development of their identities related to languages and cultures. Through these types of projects we can also showcase how the diversity of many communities provides opportunities rather than problems, and how the constant technical, political and social changes in the contemporary world can be a base for new ways of teaching and learning, rather than experiencing them as a threat to the status quo. For, in all of this, we can facilitate students' development of skills to engage in healthy, respectful, productive dialogue with people from different cultures and with different opinions.

References

Abbott, M., Brecht, R. D., Davidson, D. E., Fenstermacher, H., Fischer, D., Rivers, W. P., Slater, R., Weinberg, A. & Wiley, T. (2014). Languages for all? Final report. *European Journal of Language Policy, 6*(2), 252.

Abbott, M. G., Aronoff, M., Baird, J., Chu, D., Davidson, D. E., Dirks, N. B., Edwards, B. T., Eikenberry, K., Feal, R. G., Gluck, C., McEldowney, N., Rubin, P., Rumbaut, R. G., Tienda, M., Wallach, K. L., Wood, D. P., & Yu, P. (2017). *America's Languages: Investing in Language Education for the 21st Century.* Cambridge MA: American Academy of Arts and Sciences. https://www.amacad.org/project/commission-language-learning—accessed 19 February 2019

ACTFL (2017). NCSSFL-ACTFL Can-Do Statements for Intercultural Communication. https://www.actfl.org/publications/guidelines-and-manuals/ncssfl-actfl-can-do-statements

ACTFL Performance Descriptors for Language Learners, (2015), 2nd ed. Alexandria, VA: Author. Accessible at: https://www.actfl.org/sites/default/files/pdfs/ACTFL Performance-Descriptors.pdf

ACTFL Proficiency Guidelines (2012). Alexandria, VA: Author. Accessible at: https://www.actfl.org/sites/default/files/pdfs/public/ACTFLProficiency Guidelines2012_FINAL.pdf

ACTFL Integrated Performance Assessment Handbook, (2003). Alexandria, VA: Author. Accessible at www.actfl.org

Adair-Hauck, B., Glisan, E. W., & Troyan, F. J. (2013). *Implementing Integrated Performance Assessment.* Alexandria, VA: ACTFL.

Ashdown, P. (2012) Ted Talk. https://www.youtube.com/watch?time_continue= 960&v=zuAj2F54bdo)—accessed 19 February 2019

Barnett, R. (1997). *Higher Education: A Critical Business,* Buckingham: Society for Research into Higher Education and Open University Press.

Barrett, M. 2007, *Children's Knowledge, Beliefs and Feelings about Nations and National Groups.* Hove and New York: Psychology Press—Taylor and Francis Group.

Bayer, C. (2017). PISA 2018 Test to include global competency assessment. *Harvard Graduate School of Education, 12.* Available at https://www.gse.harvard. edu/news/17/12/pisa-2018-test-include-global-competency-assessment

Beard, M. (2017). Why Learn German? The Times Literary Supplement. August 27, 2017. https://www.the-tls.co.uk/why-learn-german/—retrieved April 2019

Beghetto, R. A. (2017). Lesson unplanning: toward transforming routine tasks into nonroutine problems. *ZDM Mathematics Education, 49,* 987-993. https://doi-org.ezproxy.lib.uconn.edu/10.1007/s11858-017-0885-1

Beghetto, R. A. (2018). *What If? Building Students' Problem-Solving Skills Through Complex Challenges: Building Students' Problem-Solving Skills Through Complex Challenges.* Alexandria, VA: ASCD.

Blodget, A. S. (2017) The unmet need for interdisciplinary education. https://www.edweek.org/ew/articles/2017/03/08/the-unmet-need-for-interdisciplinary-education.html

Bohling, A., Wagner, M., Cardetti, F., & Byram, M. (2016, week June 20th). Unit: Understanding different scenarios in immigration. *CASLS Topic of the Week: 2016-06-20, Center for Applied Second Language Studies Eugene,* OR: University of Oregon.

Bong, D. (2019). Proficiency vs. Performance vs. Achievement. Seal of Biliteracy. https://sealofbiliteracy.org/blog/proficiency-vs-performance-vs-achievement/

Byram, M. (1997). *Teaching and Assessing Intercultural Communicative Competence.* Clevedon, UK: Multilingual Matters.

Byram, M. (2008). *From Foreign Language Education to Education for Intercultural Citizenship.* Tonawanda, NY: Multilingual Matters.

Byram, M., Conlon Perugini, D. and Wagner, M. (2013) The development of Intercultural Citizenship in the elementary school Spanish classroom. *Learning Languages 18* (1), 16-31.

Byram, M., Golubeva, I., Han, H., & Wagner, M. (Eds.) (2017). *From Principles to Practice in Education for Intercultural Citizenship.* Tonawanda, NY: Multilingual Matters.

Byram, M. & Wagner, M. (2018). Making a difference: language teaching for intercultural and international dialogue. *Foreign Language Annals, 51,* 140–151.

Byram, M. and Zarate, G. (1996) Defining and assessing intercultural competence: some principles and proposals for the European context. *Language Teaching* 29(4), 239-243.

Cardetti, F., Wagner, M., and Byram, M. (2018). Intercultural Citizenship as a framework for advancing quantitative literacy across disciplinary boundaries. In: L. Tunstall, V. Piercey, & G. Karaali (Eds), *Shifting Contexts, Stable Core: Advancing Quantitative Literacy in Higher Education.* (pp.27-36). Washington, DC: Mathematical Association of America.

Center for Civic Education (2014) *National Standards for Civics and Government.* http://www.civiced.org/standards?page=stds_toc_intro—accessed 19 February 2019

Civil, M. (2002). Culture and mathematics: a community approach. *Journal of Intercultural Studies, 23,* 133-148.

Clementi, D. & Terrill, L. (2017). *The Keys to Planning for Learning: Effective Curriculum, Unit, and Lesson Design.* (Second Edition). Alexandria, VA: American Council on the Teaching of Foreign Languages.

Coffey, H. (2009). *Justification for Interdisciplinary Teaching.* Retrieved from www.learnnc.org/lp/pages/5196

Council of Europe (2001) *Common European Framework of Reference for Languages: learning, teaching assessment.* Strasbourg: Council of Europe. www.coe.int/lang-cefr—accessed 18 February 2019

Council of Europe (2018) *Companion Volume to the Common European Framework of Reference for Languages.* Strasbourg: Council of Europe. www.coe.int/en/web/common-european-framework-reference-languages—accessed 18 February 2019

Council of Europe (2018). *Reference Framework of Competences for Democratic Culture.* https://www.coe.int/en/web/education/competences-for-democratic-culture—accessed September 2018

Coyle, D. (2007). Content and language integrated learning: toward a connected research agenda for CLIL pedagogies. *International Journal of Bilingual Education and Bilingualism, 10*(5), 543-562.

Curriculum 21: Mapping the global classroom of the future. Retrieved from http://www.curriculum21.com/

Davies, A. (2003). *The Native Speaker. Myth and Reality.* Clevedon: Multilingual Matters.

Dewey, J. (1929). *The Quest for Certainty: A Study of the Relation of Knowledge and Action.* London: George Allen and Unwin.

Ennser–Kananen, J. (2016). A Pedagogy of Pain: New Directions for World Language Education. *The Modern Language Journal, 100*(2), 556-564.

Fantini, A. (2018). *Intercultural communicative competence in educational exchange: A multinational perspective.* New York, NY: Routledge.

Firn, G. (2018). Bringing the 5 Cs into your classroom. *eSchool News: Daily Tech News & Innovation.* Retrieved from https://www.eschoolnews.com/2018/04/19/bringing-5cs-classroom/

Frankenstein, M. (1990). Incorporating race, gender, and class issues into a critical Mathematical Literacy curriculum. *The Journal of Negro Education, 59*(3), 336-347.

Freire, P. (1993). *Pedagogy of the Oppressed.* New York: Continuum.

Garrett Rucks, P. (2013). A Discussion Based Online Approach to Fostering Deep Cultural Inquiry in an Introductory Language Course. *Foreign Language Annals, 46*(2), 191-212.

Glisan, E. W., & Donato, R. (2012). Guest editors' message. *Foreign Language Annals, 45*(s1), s3-s7.

Global Peace Path (n.d.) https://www.tefl.anglistik.uni-muenchen.de/projects-events/globalpeacepath/index.html—accessed January 2019

Glynn, C., Wesely, P. & Wassell, B. (2014). *Words and Actions: Teaching Languages Through the Lens of Social Justice.* Alexandria, VA: The American Council on the Teaching of Foreign Languages.

Grabe, W. & Stoller, F. L. (1997). Content-based instruction: research foundations. In: M. Snow and D. Brinton (Eds.), *The Content-Based Classroom: Perspectives on Integrating Language and Content* (pp. 5-21). White Plains, NY: Longman.

Gonzalez, L. (2009). Teaching mathematics for social justice: reflections on a community of practice for urban high school mathematics teachers. *Journal of Urban Mathematics Education, 2*(1), 22-51.

Grasso, D., & Burkins, M. (Eds.). (2010). *Holistic Engineering Education: Beyond Technology.* Springer Science & Business Media.

Gutstein, E. (2003). Teaching and learning mathematics for social justice in an urban, Latino school. *Journal for Research in Mathematics Education, 34*(1), 37-73.

Gutstein, E. (2006). *Reading and Writing the World with Mathematics: Toward Pedagogy for Social Justice.* New York: Routledge.

Hardiman, M., S. Magsamen, G. McKhann, and J. Eilber. (2009). *Neuroeducation: Learning, Arts, and the Brain.* New York/Washington, DC: Dana.

Hoffman, E. (1989). *Lost in Translation. A Life in a New Language.* New York: Penguin Books.

Hogan, M. P. (2008). The tale of two Noras: how a Yup'ik middle schooler was differently constructed as a math learner. *Diaspora, Indigenous, and Minority Education, 2*(2), 90–114.

Jester, T. (2002). Healing the "unhealthy native": Encounters with standards-based education in Alaska. *Journal of American Indian Education, 4*(3), 1–21

Larsen Freeman, D. (2018). Looking ahead: future directions in, and future research into, Second Language Acquisition. *Foreign Language Annals, 51*(1), 55-72.

Leonard, J. (2009). "Still not saved:" The power of mathematics to liberate the oppressed. In: D. B. Martin (Ed.), *Mathematics Teaching, Learning, and Liberation in the Lives of Black Children* (pp. 304-330). New York: Routledge.

Lynch, M. P., Johnson, C. R., Sheff, N., & Gunn, H. (n.d.) Intellectual Humility in Public Discourse. https://humilityandconviction.uconn.edu/wp-content/uploads/sites/1877/2016/09/IHPD-Literature-Review-revised.pdf—accessed January 2019

Malloy, C. E. (2010). Looking throughout the world for democratic access to mathematics. In: L.D. English (Ed.), *Handbook of International Research in Mathematics Education* (pp. 34-45). New York: Routledge.

Martin, D. B. (2009). Liberating the production of knowledge about African American children and mathematics. In: D. B. Martin (Ed.), *Mathematics Teaching, Learning, and Liberation in the Lives of Black Children* (pp. 3-38). New York: Routledge.

May, S. (Ed.). (2013). *The multilingual turn: Implications for SLA, TESOL, and bilingual education.* New York, NY: Routledge.

McTighe, J., Wiggins, G. (n.d.). Books: Essential Questions. ASCD. Retrieved from http://www.ascd.org/publications/books/109004/chapters/What-Makes-a-Question-Essential%A2.aspx

Meredith, B., Geyer, M & Wagner, M. (2018). Social justice in beginning language instruction: interpreting fairy tales. *SCOLT Dimensions 2018* http://www.scolt.org/images/PDFs/dimension/2018/5_Dimension2018.pdf.—accessed January 2019

Met, M. (1998). Curriculum decision-making in content-based language teaching. In: J. Cenoz and F. Genesee (Eds.) *Beyond Bilingualism. Multilingualism and Multilingual Education* (pp. 35-63). Clevedon: Multilingual Matter.

Moeller, A. J., & Abbott, M. G. (2018). Creating a new normal: Language education for all. *Foreign Language Annals, 51*(1), 12-23.

Morgan, C. (2014). Social theory in Mathematics Education: guest editorial. *Educational Studies in Mathematics, 87*(2), 123-128.

Moses, R. P. & Cobb, C.E. (2001). *Radical Equations: Civil Rights from Mississippi to the Algebra Project. Boston:* Beacon Press.

National Academies of Sciences, Engineering, and Medicine. 2018. *The Integration of the Humanities and Arts with Sciences, Engineering, and Medicine in Higher Education: Branches from the Same Tree.* Washington, DC: The National Academies Press. doi: https://doi.org/10.17226/24988.

National Council for the Social Studies [NCSS-C3]. (2013). *The College, Career, and Civic Life (C3) Framework for Social Studies State Standards: Guidance for Enhancing the Rigor of K-12 Civics, Economics, Geography, and History.* Silver Spring, MD: NCSS.

National Curriculum for Social Studies [NCSS]. (2010). *National Council for the Social Studies, Expectations of Excellence: Curriculum Standards for Social Studies.* Washington, D.C.: NCSS.

National Education Association. (2012). *Preparing 21st Century Students for a Global Society: An Educator's Guide to the "Four Cs."* Alexandria, VA: National Education Association.

National Governors Association Center for Best Practices and Council of Chief State School Officers. [CCSSM] (2010). *Common Core State Standards for Mathematics.* Washington, DC: CCSS.

National Governors Association Center for Best Practices and Council of Chief State School Officers. [CCSS-ELA] (2010). *Common Core State Standards for English, Language, Arts.* Washington, DC: CCSS.

NGSS Lead States (2013). Next Generation Science Standards: For States, By States. Washington, DC: The National Academies Press.

National Research Council [NRC]. (2002). Adding it up: helping children learn mathematics. In: J. Kilpatrick, J. Swafford, & B. Findell (Eds.). *Mathematics Learning Study Committee, Center for Education, Division of Behavioral and Social Sciences and Education.* Washington, DC: National Academy Press.

National Research Council [NRC Framework]. (2012). *A Framework for K-12 Science Education: Practices, Crosscutting Concepts, and Core Ideas.* Committee on a Conceptual Framework for New K-12 Science Education Standards. Board on Science Education, Division of Behavioral and Social Sciences and Education. Washington, DC: The National Academies Press.

National Science Foundation (n.d.) *What is Interdisciplinary Research?* https://www.nsf.gov/od/oia/additional_resources/interdisciplinary_research/definition.jsp—accessed January 2019

National Standards Collaborative Board (2015). *World-Readiness Standards for Learning Languages.* (4th ed.). Alexandria, VA: American Council on the Teaching of Foreign Languages.

Nieto, S. (2010). *Language, culture, and teaching: Critical perspectives.* New York, NY: Routledge.

Nieto, S. (n.d.). Diversity Education: Lessons For A Just World. *Rozenberg Quarterly: The Magazine.* Retrieved from http://rozenbergquarterly.com/diversity-education-lessons-for-a-just-world-sonia-nieto/

Oakes, J., Joseph, R. & Muir, K. (2004). Access and achievement in mathematics and science: Inequalities that endure and change. In: J. A. Banks & C.A. Banks, (Eds.), *Handbook of Research on Multicultural Education* (2nd ed., pp. 69-90). San Francisco: Jossey-Bass.

Osborn, T. A. (2006). *Teaching World Languages for Social Justice: A Sourcebook of Principles and Practices.* Mahwah, NJ: Lawrence Erlbaum Associates.

Phakeng, M., Halai, A., Valero, P., Wagner, D., & Walshaw, M. (2014). The calculus of social change: Mathematics at the cutting edge. *Proceedings of PME38 and PME-NA36, 1,* 55-83.

Piccardo, E. (2014). *From Communicative to Action-Oriented: A Research Pathway.* Toronto, ON: Curriculum Services Canada.

Rauschert, P. & Byram, M. (2018). Service-learning and Intercultural Citizenship in foreign language education, *Cambridge Journal of Education,* 48 (3) 353-369 doi: 10.1080/0305764X.2017.1337722

Reagan, T. G. & Osborn, T. A. (2002). *The Foreign Language Educator in Society: Toward a Critical Pedagogy.* London: Routledge.

Risager, K. (2006). *Language and Culture. Global Flows and Local Complexity.* Clevedon, UK: Multilingual Matters.

Rivers, W.P., Robinson, J.P., Harwood, P.G. & Brecht, R.D. (2013) Language Votes: Attitudes Toward Foreign Language Policies. *Foreign Language Annals 46*(3) 329-338

Rivers, W. P. & Brecht, R. D. (2018). America's languages: The future of language advocacy. *Foreign Language Annals, 51*(1), 24-34.

Root-Bernstein, R. & Root-Bernstein, M. (1999). *Sparks of Genius: The Thirteen Thinking Tools of the World's Most Creative People.* Boston and New York: Houghton Mifflin.

Sandrock, P. (2010). *The Keys to Assessing Language Performance: Teacher's Manual.* Alexandria, VA: American Council on the Teaching of Foreign Languages.

Shen, J., Jiang, S. & Liu, O. L. (2015). Reconceptualizing a college science learning experience in the new digital era: A review of literature. In: X. Ge, D. Ifenthaler, and J. Spector (Eds.) *Emerging Technologies for STEAM Education: Full Steam Ahead.* (pp. 61-79). Switzerland: Springer.

Sleeter, C. E. (1997). Mathematics, multicultural education and professional development. *Journal for Research in Mathematics Education, 28*(6), 680-696

Street, B. (1993). Culture is a verb. In D. Graddol, L. Thompson and M. Byram (Eds.) *Language and Culture,* (pp. 23-43). Clevedon, UK: Multilingual Matters/ British Association of Applied Linguistics.

Swender, E., & Duncan, G. (1998). ACTFL performance guidelines for K 12 learners. Foreign Language Annals, 31(4), 479-491.

Tanesini, A. (2018). Intellectual servility and timidity. *Journal of Philosophical Research,* 43, 21-41. doi:10.5840/jpr201872120

Tate, W. F. (1995). Returning to the root: A culturally relevant approach to mathematics pedagogy. *Theory Into Practice, 34*(3), 166-173.

Tedick, D. J., & Walker, C. L. (1994). Second language teacher education: The problems that plague us. *The Modern Language Journal, 78*(3), 300-312.

Toth, P. D., & Moranski, K. (2018). Why haven't we solved instructed SLA? A sociocognitive account. *Foreign Language Annals, 51*(1), 73-89.

Turner, E. E., & Strawhun, B. T. F. (2005). "With math, it's like you have more defense": Students investigate overcrowding at their school. In: E. Gutstein & B. Peterson (Eds.), *Rethinking Mathematics: Teaching Social Justice by the Numbers* (pp. 81-87). Milwaukee, WI: Rethinking Schools.

UNESCO (1996) *Learning: the Treasure Within. Report to UNESCO of the International Commission on Education for the Twenty-first century; Jacques Delors, Chairman.* Paris: UNESCO.

VanPatten, B. (2017). *While We're on the Topic: BVP on Language, Acquisition, and Classroom Practice.* Alexandria, VA: American Council on the Teaching of Foreign Languages.

Wagner, M., Cardetti, F., and Byram, M. (2016). Developing Intercultural Communicative Competence in the World Language Classroom and Beyond. *InterCom. Center for Applied Second Language Studies:* University of Oregon. Content No. 21294.

Wagner, M., Conlon Perugini, D. & Byram, M. (Eds.) (2018). *Teaching Intercultural Competence Across the Age Range: Theory and Practice.* Bristol, UK: Multilingual Matters.

Wagner, M., Cardetti, F. and Byram, M. (2018) The humble linguist: interdisciplinary perspectives on teaching and assessing Intercultural Citizenship. In: E. Luef and M. Marin (Eds.) *The Talking Species: Perspectives on the Evolutionary, Neuronal and Cultural Foundations of Language.* (pp. 419-443). Graz, Austria: Unipress.

Wagner, M., and Tracksdorf, N. (2018). ICC Online: Fostering the Development of Intercultural Competence in Virtual Language Classrooms (University Students). In: M. Wagner, D. Perugini, and M. Byram (Eds.) *Teaching Intercultural Competence Across the Age Range: Theory and Practice* (pp. 135-154). Bristol, UK & Blue Ridge Summit, PA: Multilingual Matters.

Wallace, D. & Tamborello Noble, J. (2018). Diverse perspectives of the immigrant experience. In: M. Wagner, D. Perugini & M. Byram (Eds.) *Teaching Intercultural Competence Across the Age Range: Theory and Practice* (pp. 94-112). Bristol, UK & Blue Ridge Summit, PA: Multilingual Matters.

Warner, C., & Dupuy, B. (2018). Moving toward multiliteracies in foreign language teaching: Past and present perspectives... and beyond. *Foreign Language Annals, 51*(1), 116-128.

Whitcomb, D., Battaly, H., Baehr, J., & Howard Snyder, D. (2017). Intellectual humility: Owning our limitations. *Philosophy and Phenomenological Research, 94*(3), 509-539.

Wiggins, G. P. & McTighe, J. (2005). *Understanding by Design.* Alexandria, VA: ASCD.

Young, H. (2014). Do young people care about learning foreign languages? *The Guardian,* US edition, Fri 7 Nov 2014 02.33 EST. Available at https://www.theguardian.com/education/2014/nov/07/-sp-do-young-people-care-about-learning-foreign-languages-data

Yulita, L. & Porto, M. (2017) Human Rights education in Foreign Language teaching: students as transformative intellectuals. In: M. Byram, I. Golubeva, Han, H. & M. Wagner (Eds.) *From Principles to Practice in Education for Intercultural Citizenship* (pp. 225-250). Bristol, UK & Blue Ridge Summit, PA: Multilingual Matters.

Appendix For Chapter 3

Appendix 3.1: Assessment by indicators and levels

Until recently, educationists have had few or no resources to assess Intercultural Competence, which would be comparable to ACTFL's levels of language competence and the indicators that define them. This has now changed in both the USA and Europe. In the USA are the *NCSSFL-ACTFL Can-Do Statements for Intercultural Communication,* discussed in detail in Chapter 2. In Europe, a new *Companion Volume to the Common European Framework of Reference for Languages* (www.coe.int/en/web/common-european-framework-reference-languages) provides indicators of 'pluricultural competence' at six levels (A1 to C2) and its use, for example, in different kinds of mediation activities. Here is an example from the level B2:

"Building on a pluricultural competence"—B2

- Can identify and reflect on similarities and differences in culturally-determined behavior patterns (e.g., gestures and speech volume) and discuss their significance in order to negotiate mutual understanding.

- Can, in an intercultural encounter, recognize that what one normally takes for granted in a particular situation is not necessarily shared by others, and can react and express him/herself appropriately.

- Can generally interpret cultural cues appropriately in the culture concerned.

- Can reflect on and explain particular ways of communicating in his/her own and other cultures, and the risks of misunderstanding they generate.

- Can generally act conventionally regarding posture, eye contact, and distance from others.

- Can generally respond appropriately to the most commonly used cultural cues.

- Can explain features of his/her own culture to members of another culture or explain features of the other culture to members of his/her own culture.

Another development in Europe is the creation of a Reference Framework of Competences for Democratic Culture (RFCDC) that includes 'competences in intercultural dialogue,' that is, 20 competences of knowledge, skills, attitudes and values. Each has indicators at three levels. Some of the competences are familiar to language teachers but formulated in a different way, such as 'Skills of Listening and Observing':

- Basic level of proficiency
  - Listens attentively to other people
  - Listens carefully to differing opinions

- Intermediate level of proficiency
  - Can listen effectively in order to decipher another person's meanings and intentions
  - Watches speakers' gestures and general body language to help himself/herself to figure out the meaning of what they are saying
- Advanced level of proficiency
  - `Pays attention to what other people imply but do not say
  - Notices how people with other cultural affiliations react differently to the same situation.

Other competences are relevant to teaching across the curriculum and therefore particularly interesting for interdisciplinary teaching. For example, in the Chapter 1 scenarios, students are engaged in what in the RFCDC is called 'civic-mindedness,' described at three levels as follows:

- Basic level of proficiency
  - Expresses a willingness to cooperate and work with others
  - Collaborates with other people for common interest causes

- Intermediate level of proficiency
  - Expresses commitment to not being a bystander when the dignity and rights of others are violated
  - Discusses what can be done to help make the community a better place

- Advanced level of proficiency
  - Exercises the obligations and responsibilities of active citizenship at the local, national or global level
  - Takes action to stay informed about civic issues

Here you will notice indicators that can be applied to the activities of students in their communities. These indicators have been validated in a careful scientific process.

Comparaison des problèmes d'eau dans chaque région [Comparing the water <u>issues</u> in each region]
Problèmes de région 1: [Region 1 issue(s)]
Problèmes de région 2: [Region 2 issue(s)]

Perspectives de comparaison [Comparison of angles]	Comment les problèmes sont... [How are the issues...]			Raisonnement (Pourquoi?) [Rationale (Why?)]
	Similaires [Similar]	**Différents** [Different]	**Surprenants** [Surprising]	
Culturel [Cultural]				
Géographique [Geographical]				
Accès [Access]				
Impact (humain, naturel, capital etc.) [Impact (human, natural, capital, etc.)]				
Autre [Other]				

Comparaison des efforts d'amélioration de la situation dans chaque région [Comparing the efforts to improve the situation in each region]
Efforts dans la région 1: [Efforts in Region 1]
Efforts dans la région 1: [Efforts in Region 2]

Perspectives de comparaison [Comparison of angles]	Comment les problèmes sont... [How are the approaches...]			Raisonnement (Pourquoi?) [Rationale (Why?)]
	Similaires [Similar]	**Différents** [Different]	**Surprenants** [Surprising]	
Culturel [Cultural]				
Géographique [Geographical]				
Accès [Access]				
Ressources (humaines, naturelles, capitales,...) [Resources (human, natural, capital, ...)]				

Comment pouvons-nous améliorer la situation [How can we improve the situation]				
Plan d'actions possibles [Possible action plans]	**Comment ces actions sont-elles soutenues par vos connaissances des différentes matières?** [How are these actions supported by what you know from the different subjects]			
	Langues [Languages]	**Sciences sociales** [Social studies]	**Sciences naturelles** [Sciences]	**Mathématiques** [Mathematics]
Action 1 **Que peut faire notre communauté?** [What can our community do?] **Plan de diffusion** [Dissemination plan]				
Action 2 **Que peut faire notre communauté?** [What can our community do?] **Plan de diffusion** [Dissemination plan]				
Action 3				

Appendix 3.3: Template to guide planning of interdisciplinary Intercultural Citizenship unit

Preliminary Considerations

How will your lessons provide students opportunities to...

...acquire new knowledge and understanding of products, perspectives and practices related to the topic/theme?	
...discover for themselves the practices of people in other contexts?	▶▶▶

....compare and contrast perspectives in different contexts on the issue in question?

...analyze and evaluate products and perspectives that influence practices and vice versa?

...take or plan informed action in their (local, national, or international) community?

How will the lesson be...

...goal-focused?

...learner-centered?

...brain-based?

How will the lesson provide opportunities for...

...critical thinking and problem-solving?

...creativity?

...collaboration?

...communication?

...assessment/feedback?

▶▶▶

Theme for the Unit

Is your theme versatile enough to...

...use and advance understanding specific to each subject area/discipline involved?	
...allow the application of knowledge acquired in one subject/discipline to another, each enhanced by the other?	
...prompt students to reflect on and challenge their own and others' ideas using the interdisciplinary perspective and their own experiences?	
...allow for rich collaborative learning opportunities for students of different cultural backgrounds to grapple with and critically analyze contemporary societal issues, in their historical development, and problems of local and global concern using an interdisciplinary approach?	

Unit Interdisciplinary Purpose and Learning Objectives

Interdisciplinary purpose	
Interdisciplinary learning objectives	

Assessment Plans

Formative assessments

▶▶▶

Summative assessments

Core Activities

Activity 1	
Activity 2	
Culminating Activity	

Discipline-Specific Contributions, Learning Objectives, Curriculum Standards

Languages classroom

Contributions	
Learning objectives	
Standards addressed	

▶▶▶

Subject 2	
Contributions	
Learning objectives	
Standards addressed	

Subject 3	
Contributions	
Learning objectives	
Standards addressed	

Subject 4	
Contributions	
Learning objectives	
Standards addressed	

[1] Clementi & Terrill (2017, p. 68)

Appendix For Chapter 4

Appendix 4.1: Activity and guiding questions for group work

Sample instructions for the poster creation

Based on this investigation, prepare a poster in Spanish that helps others to understand and learn about this disaster. The poster should include: name, place, and date; affected area relative to the state of Connecticut; preparation plans; and the logotype you created. Don't forget to include the sources of information that support the contents of your poster.

Sample guiding questions for the exploration in the TL and in English

Note that the questions are composed of many cognates for speakers of English

Las siguientes preguntas e instrucciones servirán para guiar a tu grupo a explorar los desastres naturales que suelen afectar a nuestra localidad.

- ¿Cuáles son los desastres naturales que han ocurrido en nuestra localidad?

- Elige uno de los desastres y averigua: la fecha, el área afectada, ¿cómo se compara ese área en relación a todo el estado y en relación al país? averigua otros datos generales que sean importantes para el desastre que tu grupo ha elegido.

- Explica en qué consiste este tipo de desastre, cuán frecuentemente ocurre en nuestra area (fechas), y qué lugares han sido más afectados por este desastre dentro de nuestro estado.

- Describe planes de preparación existen para este tipo de desastre.

- Diseña un logotipo que sirva para identificar y distinguir el desastre natural que ustedes han elegido. Deben asegurarse que el logotipo representa características específicas de su desastre.

- ¡Todos los miembros del grupo deben participar!

The following questions and prompts will guide your group's exploration of natural disasters that have affected our local area or community.

- Which natural disasters have occurred in our local area or community?

- Choose one of them and investigate the following: date, affected area, how the area compares to that of our state and to the country.

- Find out other general information important for the disaster you chose.

- Explain what this type of disaster comprises, how frequently it occurs in our local area (dates), and which places have been affected by such a disaster within our state.
- Describe any preparation plans that exist for this type of disasters
- Design a logo (logotype) that helps identify and distinguish the characteristics of this disaster. Make sure your logo represents the specific characteristics of your disaster.
- Make sure all members of your group participate!

Discussion of findings: Discover and Interact

"Natural Disaster in our community/local area"

	Uno de los desastres naturales que ocurrió en nuestra localidad fue...	Este desastre se parece al de nuestro grupo porque...	Lo más impresionante de este desastre fue... Esto me impresionó porque....
Report 1	Nombre del desastre: Lugar más afectado: Fecha:	Fíjate en los elementos característicos: agua, vientos, fuego, tierra. Encuentras alguna similitud en el plan de preparación? Compara el área total afectada en relación al estado y al país	
Sample answers	■ Huracan Irene ■ East Haven ■ August, 2012	Este huracán también tuvo vientos fuertes; Las personas también protegieron sus ventanas con maderas; los daños también costaron más de $1 millón	Casi todo el estado de Connecticut perdió luz. Esto me impresionó porque TODOS fuimos afectados con este desastre.

Sample guiding questions to facilitate whole-group discussion

Analyze the natural disasters that other groups investigated and compare their results with your group's results. The table and the following questions will facilitate your group's conversation about your findings from the gallery walk:

- Are there any disasters with characteristics similar to yours? Which characteristics are those?
- Which is the most common disaster in our local area?

- Is there any disaster that had a similar impact on the whole state as the one your group investigated? Why do you think this is so?

- Which disaster that had the largest impact on the whole state? Why do you think this is so?

- Did any of the other disasters have a similar preparation plan to yours? Why do you think this is so?

- Did any of the other disasters have a more developed preparation plan to yours? Why do you think this is so?

Instructions for group conversation:
- Compare your responses to your fellow group members. If there are differences between your observations, talk about these to understand why you have different answers. Did others pay attention to something you did not? Where there things important to you that others did not consider? Do you understand your fellow group member's point of view? Do they understand yours?

Appendix 4.2: Suggested extension to natural disasters around the world

Guiding questions for students' investigation of natural disaster somewhere else in the world

- Which disasters have occurred in the area that you have been assigned?

- For each type of disaster, investigate the following: what is it about, its frequency, date(s), the affected area, how does the affected area compare to the entire state and to the whole country, include any other relevant information.

- What is the existing preparation plan for this type of disasters?

- Chose an appropriate logotype for this disaster.

- All members of the group should participate.

Extending to other subjects: Reflection
Students write an individual reflection that connects their understanding of dissasters in other parts of the word with what they are learning in other subjects (e.g., geology). This activity is a high-level cognitive activity in which students analyze and synthesize their understandings. Much of the vocabulary is either recycled from previous activities or consists of cognates (e.g., geology).

Example: Mexico is bounded by the Pacific Ocean on the West and South and by the Gulf of Mexico on the East. This contributes to the occurrence of cyclones in this country. The situation is similar in Cuba that is surrounded by the ocean and where cyclones are common too.

Appendix 4.3: Chart for interpretation/comparison across groups to guide synthesis report

	Uno de los desastres naturales que ocurrió en nuestra localidad fue...	Este desastre se parece al de nuestro grupo porque...	Lo más impresionante de este desastre fue... Esto me impresionó porque....
Report 1	Nombre del desastre: Lugar más afectado: Fecha:	Fíjate en los elementos característicos: agua, vientos, fuego, tierra. Encuentras alguna similitud en el plan de preparación? Compara el área total afectada en relación al estado y al país	
Sample answers	■ Huracan Irene ■ East Haven ■ August, 2012	Este huracán también tuvo vientos fuertes; Las personas también protegieron sus ventanas con maderas; los daños también costaron más de $1 millón	Casi todo el estado de Connecticut perdió luz. Esto me impresionó porque TODOS fuimos afectados con este desastre.

Appendix 4.4: Overview of timeline and suggestions for materials

Week 1

- Assessment of related vocabulary and background knowledge related to unit (family, housing, weather, work, migration, etc.)
- Pre-assessment of perspectives on natural disasters
- Introduction of natural disasters (group work, and each group just checks in a little more detail)

Suggested resources specific to natural disasters:

- Resources to reactivate and introduce vocabulary related to natural disasters:
- A Quizlet set of vocabulary for natural disasters (https://quizlet.com/18508325/spanish-natural-disasters-vocab-flash-cards/)
- An online slideshow with vocabulary (https://study.com/academy/lesson/spanish-terms-for-natural-disasters-emergencies.html)
- Resources for pre-assessment: Video images of the aftermath of Hurricane Maria https://www.sandiegouniontribune.com/opinion/the-conversation/sd-hurricane-maria-puerto-rico-20170920-htmlstory.html

- Resources with general information about natural disasters in Spanish to guide the group work: http://www.geoenciclopedia.com/desastres-naturales/
- See also Appendix XX: Guiding questions for group work

Week 2

- Introduction of eventual project
- Groups investigate different questions related to Hurricane Maria
- Start planning what information will be important to present
- Interview witnesses or friends and relatives of witnesses in the region

Suggested resources for different perspectives specific to Hurricane Maria:

- News article showcasing Hurricane Maria in numbers and pictures: https://www.univision.com/puerto-rico/wlii/noticias/huracan-maria/en-numeros-oficiales-y-fotos-asi-va-la-recuperacion-de-puerto-rico-a-un-mes-de-maria-segun-el-gobierno-fotos
- Impact of Hurricane Maria on housing: https://www.elnuevodia.com/noticias/locales/nota/elhuracanmariadestruyo70000viviendasenpuertorico-2374555/
- Effects of Hurricane Maria on labor market https://www.elnuevodia.com/negocios/economia/nota/elhuracanmariaprovocounacatastrofeenelmercadolaboral-2374303/
- Video in Spanish illustrating and modeling how to use the data in meaningful ways: https://www.youtube.com/watch?v=hhUvtP-hOgQ

Week 3

- Continue investigation
- Based on their investigations and interviews, groups formulate a possible action plan relevant to their community or region
- Prepare presentation of findings

Suggested resources for further investigation, potential action plans, and support presentations:

- Articles from local media news
- Federal information about preparation plans for hurricanes and other disasters, recovery assistance, and volunteer opportunities: https://www.fema.gov/es
- Spanish material from FEMA on preparation plans: https://www.fema.gov/media-library/assets/documents/93453

Week 4

- Present findings to other groups
- Students write reports to summarize what they have learned
- Groups work on synthesis of information

Suggested resources for learning from others:

- See Appendix 4.3: Focused chart for interpretation and comparison across groups to guide synthesis report

Week 5:

- Plan event: Invite participants, review logistics, obtain permissions (principal?)
- Plan advertisement scheme: prepare handouts, pamphlets, posters, or webpage....

Week 6

- Prepare presentation: What are the effects still today of Hurricane Maria? (different groups present different parts)

Index